D0600874

PEACHES and other juicy fruits

From Sweet to Savory — 150 Recipes for Peaches, Plums, Nectarines, and Apricots

Olwen Woodier

Storey Publishing

The mission of Storey Publishing is to serve our customers by publishing practical information that encourages personal independence in harmony with the environment.

Edited by Dianne M. Cutillo, Carey L. Boucher, and Siobhan Dunn
Art direction and cover design by Lisa Clark
Cover photograph © Silver Visions Publishing Co., Inc./Stock Food America; back cover © John Foxx/Alamy
Text design and production by Susi Oberhelman, Melanie Jolicoeur, and Kelley Nesbit
Indexed by Susan Olason, Indexes & Knowledge Maps

The following recipes are from *Simply Bishop's: Easy Seasonal Recipes* (Copyright © 2002 by John Bishop and Dennis Green. Published by Douglas & McIntyre Ltd. Reprinted by permission of the publisher.) Bishop's Chilled Peach and Honey Soup, page 63; Bishop's Chilled Plum Soup with Tarragon, page 64; Bishop's Split Roast Chicken with Pickled Peaches, page 113; Bishop's Roast Pork Tenderloin with Apricot and Sage Stuffing, page 114; Bishop's Poached Peaches or Apricots, page 133; Bishop's Chèvre Cheesecake with Apricot Brandy Syrup, page 160.

Copyright © 2004 by Olwen Woodier
Illustrations © John Burgoyne

All rights reserved. No part of this book may be reproduced without written permission from the publisher, except by a reviewer who may quote brief passages or reproduce illustrations in a review with appropriate credits; nor may any part of this book be reproduced, stored in a retrieval system, or transmitted in any form or by any means — electronic, mechanical, photocopying, recording, or other — without written permission from the publisher.

The information in this book is true and complete to the best of our knowledge. All recommendations are made without guarantee on the part of the author or Storey Publishing. The author and publisher disclaim any liability in connection with the use of this information. For additional information please contact Storey Publishing, 210 MASS MoCA Way, North Adams, MA 01247.

Storey books are available for special premium and promotional uses and for customized editions. For further information, please call 1-800-793-9396.

Printed in the United States by Von Hoffmann
10 9 8 7 6 5 4 3 2 1

Library of Congress Cataloging-in-Publication Data

Woodier, Olwen
  Peaches and other juicy fruits : From Sweet to Savory — 150 recipes for peaches, plums, nectarines, and apricots / Olwen Woodier.
      p. cm.
    Includes index.
    ISBN 1-58017-499-X (alk. paper)
    1. Cookery (Stone fruit) I. Title.
  TX813.S85W66 2004
  641.6'42—dc22
                                                                2004001520

Contents

Preface

HOW SWEET ARE THE FLAVORS OF SUMMER! This is a season of great anticipation, when we eagerly reach to pluck and savor sun-ripened fruits from our own gardens and from local farms and orchards. While there are numerous stars of summer, the cream of the crop for many of us are those bursting with the essential fragrance and flavor — sweet as honey — of tree-ripened apricots, peaches, nectarines, and plums. Who hasn't experienced the ecstasy that comes after biting into a sun-warmed peach? A perfectly ripe nectarine? A fat, juicy plum? All it takes is one bite to release a stream of nectar that tastes like nothing else, except, perhaps, what must be the essence of summer.

Before, however, we are treated to the heady ripeness of local peaches and nectarines, which appear in late June, we may be lucky enough to find their earlier fruiting kin, the smaller, soft-fleshed apricots. About the same size and shape of some plum varieties — which we start seeing sometime in August, right in the middle of the glut of peaches and nectarines — apricots appear in late May. Though apricots don't stream with juice, those that are tree-ripened exude a delicate aroma that gives little hint of the sweet, almost tangy, succulent flesh lying beneath velvety golden, pink-flushed skin. Today, we can enjoy the new specialty stone fruits that are hybrid crosses of plums and apricots and peaches and plums, as well as newer and sweeter hybrid crosses of white and yellow peaches. And all of these fruits — whether fresh, frozen, or preserved — lend themselves to preparations for delicious meals and snacks during summer or any other time of year.

Acknowledgments

To my mother, Joyse Astbury Woodier, who is one of the happiest and feistiest ladies I have known and who, at 95, continues to be a source of great inspiration. Thank you, Mum.

Thanks to my husband, Richard Busch, who kept the home fires stoked by becoming chief shopper and running a zillion errands to help me meet my deadlines.

It takes so many people to create a book — from planting the seed, to grooming the blooms, to harvesting the fruits.

I thank editors Dianne Cutillo for planting and nurturing the seed, Carey Boucher for her careful weeding, Siobhan Dunn and Doris Troy for the final grooming; and designers Susi Oberhelman, Melanie Jolicoeur, and Kelley Nesbit and art director Lisa Clark for harvesting the fruits of all our labors.

I also give special thanks to editorial director Deborah Balmuth, whose confidence in me helped bring this book to fruition.

In advance, I thank Storey publicity and marketing/sales people for their talented efforts in bringing this and my other books into the public eye. They belong to the most dedicated group I have ever enjoyed working with.

I also want to thank those people who were generous with their time and allowed me to interview them and/or shared recipes with me: Grower Steve Brenkwitz and his wife, Mary Anne, of Eden Garden Farm, Tracy, California; Michael Kramer, owner/executive chef of McCrady's Restaurant, Charleston, South Carolina; John Bishop, owner/ executive chef of Bishop's Restaurant in Vancouver, British Columbia; Kate Zurschmeide of Great Country Farms, Bluemont, Virginia; Madelaine Sosnitsky, owner of Eiffel Tower Restaurant, Leesburg, Virginia; Julio Fuentes, owner/chef of La Chocita Grill, Leesburg, Virginia; and Mark Rieger, professor of horticulture at the University of Georgia.

I am also indebted to the various stone fruit associations and councils that are listed in the Resources section on page 181.

Thank you; this book wouldn't have happened without you.

ABOUT THE FRUITS

Apricots, cherries, nectarines, peaches, and plums number
among the world's favorite fruits and have for close to 5,000
years, ever since they were carried to far areas of the globe
from their ancient origins in Asia.

Peaches and Nectarines
(Prunus persica)

The nectarine is a smooth-skin variation of the peach, which is second only to the apple in popularity in North America. The skin and flesh of both peaches and nectarines may be white or yellow, sometimes heavily splashed with red, surrounding a furrowed freestone or clingstone pit.

Peaches and nectarines originated in China nearly 3,000 years ago and were transported into the Middle East, northern Africa, and Rome via trading routes. On their conquering marches, the Romans introduced the fruits to the rest of Europe. The peach reached northeast American shores in 1629, when the governor of the Massachusetts Bay Colony ordered peach stones from England. The Spanish, who had introduced them into the New World during the 1500s, were the first to plant peaches in Florida and California, in the early 1600s. It was the Native Americans, however, who spread them across North America by planting them wherever they moved.

Today, peaches and nectarines are cultivated commercially in 15 states. The major growers are in the San Joaquin Valley, California, which produces more than 90 percent of nectarines and approximately 60 percent of peaches in the United States. The fruits are also grown in South Carolina, Georgia, New Jersey, Pennsylvania, Virginia, Ohio, Michigan, and New York. The harvest starts in early May in California, where the cooler summer temperatures delay the ripening process, and continues through early October.

While there are many new and wonderful freestone yellow-fleshed peaches on the market, some of the old-time favorites and their hybrids (Elberta, Haven, and Crest varieties) are still favored by commercial growers. The older white-fleshed, sub-acid peaches, such as Babcock, Belle of Georgia, and Nectar, are exceptionally sweet and

CLINGSTONE V. FREESTONE

Peaches and nectarines fall into two groups: clingstone and freestone. Clingstone have firm flesh that clings tenaciously to the pit (stone) and can be removed only by slicing off with a knife. These firmer fruits are favored by commercial processors for drying, freezing, and canning in syrup — whole, halved, or sliced — because they hold their shape.

Freestone have juicy, soft flesh that separates easily from the pit. It's possible to split a ripe freestone by twisting it gently down the seam in opposite directions. Considered the best for eating out of hand, freestone can be sliced neatly for an attractive presentation in salads and desserts. They also speed up the cook's work when making pies, crumbles, cakes, salsas, and other recipes calling for slicing and dicing.

juicy with peachy flavor and aroma, but only when they are ripe, and at that stage they bruise easily. Commercial growers favor the new varieties of white peaches, which are very sweet when picked firm and continue to ripen off the tree.

New white-fleshed hybrids, such as Spring Snow and White Lady, are even lower in acid and higher in sugar. Summerwhite peaches and nectarines — these represent about 20 percent of the total California peach and nectarine crop — have white skin splashed with bright pink and flesh that ranges from white to light pink. All of these new-breed whites are sublimely sweet when immature and can be harvested firm and served before they are fully ripe. Compared to balanced-acid hybrids, and even the not-so-old sub-acid breeds, they have a more delicate flavor — one that is sugary rather than peachy.

Other white-fleshed nectarines with big sugary punch include any variety sporting the label "Arctic." Of course, both yellow and white nectarines are tantalizingly aromatic and flavorful when fully ripe, ranging from sugary to peachy verging on spicy plum.

Although the nectarine is a variety of peach with a recessive gene — the one that gives the peach its downy skin — it is a separate fruit. Occasionally, peach trees produce fruit with stones that grow into nectarine trees, and sometimes

DONUT PEACHES

Donut peaches are the smallest and among the sweetest of all the peach varieties. They are cling-free, measure about 3 inches in diameter and 1 inch thick, and have white flesh and pale yellow skin blushed with pinkish red. Frieda's introduced the Donut Peach to consumers in 1986, and today these special peaches are grown in California and Washington by growers under contract. Donut peaches have a short season of five to six weeks, debuting at the beginning of August. During that time they are superlatively worth seeking out.

peaches spontaneously appear on nectarine trees. Because there is no way to identify whether a nectarine stone will produce a nectarine or a peach, commercial growers graft nectarine-bearing branches onto peach trees. Those branches will continue to produce nectarines. Some pomologists say that the nectarine predates the peach. There are also those who believe that the peach developed as the result of a spontaneous cross between a nectarine and an almond.

While nectarine trees are almost identical to peach trees in size and shape, nectarine fruits tend to be slightly smaller (some are no bigger than a large plum) with smooth, shiny skin and firmer flesh. A perfectly ripe nectarine, however, can be just as sweet as a peach. The word *nectarine*, in fact, means "sweet as nectar" and comes from *nectar,* the name the Olympic gods gave to their sweet drink. You can appreciate that thought the next time you buy a can of peach nectar; you won't find nectarine nectar because the processing market for nectarines is so small that even the clingstone varieties are sold for eating fresh.

It was not until after World War II that nectarines became the succulent, juicy fruits that they are today. Before that time, they were not even yellow, but had pale skin and dry white flesh. The breakthrough came when California plant breeder Fred Anderson, a disciple of Luther Burbank, saw

PEACHES USDA Dietary Values per 100 grams raw edible portion (1 medium-sized peach)	
Water	89.1 percent
Calories	38
Protein	0.6 g
Fat	0.1 g
Carbohydrates	9.7 g
Fiber	0.6 g
Vitamin A	1,330 IU (International Units)
Thiamin, B_1	0.02 mg
Riboflavin, B_2	0.05 mg
Niacin	1 mg
Vitamin C	7 mg
Calcium	9 mg
Phosphorus	19 mg
Iron	0.5 mg
Sodium	1 mg
Potassium	202 mg

NECTARINES USDA Dietary Values per 100 grams raw edible portion (1 medium-sized nectarine)	
Water	81.8 percent
Calories	64
Protein	0.6 g
Fat	Trace
Carbohydrates	17 g
Fiber	0.4 g
Vitamin A	1,650 IU (International Units)
Thiamin, B_1	0.00
Riboflavin, B_2	0.00
Niacin	0.00
Vitamin C	13 mg
Calcium	4 mg
Phosphorus	24 mg
Iron	0.5 mg
Sodium	6 mg
Potassium	294 mg

that the way to improve nectarines was to cross them with peaches. He called his resultant offspring "Le Grand nectarine," a large, juicy, yellow-fleshed fruit that finally rivaled the peach in color, size and texture.

SELECTING AND STORING

Domestic peaches and nectarines are available for purchase from May until October. Late-season harvests can produce very sweet and juicy yellow or white fruits that have had the benefit of maturing and tree ripening during the warm summer months. Some of these late peach cultivars are September Sun, Ryan Sun, and Arctic varieties. From December until March, out-of-season peaches and nectarines are available for purchase from Chile. Nectarines and peaches (as well as plums and apricots) are interchangeable in recipes, so take advantage of these fruits when you find them in season locally.

In the supermarket, peaches, nectarines and plums may be labeled with little stickers that say "Tree Ripe." Unlike apples, however, peaches and nectarines (and most plums) are not sold by variety, so unless you buy from a local farmstand, you may never know the name of your delicious purchase.

Although it's tempting to believe that a fruit heavily blushed with red must be ripe, the red coloration is not a sign of ripeness but an indication

DRIED PEACHES AND NECTARINES

USDA Dietary Values per 100 grams uncooked dried (about ½ cup)

Dried peaches and nectarines contain twice the vitamin A and four times the potassium content of raw fruits. (*Note:* Cooking dried fruits has the effect of reverting the concentrated nutrients closer to the nutritional values of the raw fruits.)

Water	25 percent
Calories	262
Protein	3.1 g
Fat	0.7 g
Carbohydrates	68.3 g
Fiber	3.1 g
Vitamin A	3,900 IU (International Units)
Thiamin, B_1	0.01 mg
Riboflavin, B_2	0.19 mg
Niacin	5.3 mg
Vitamin C	18 mg
Calcium	48 mg
Phosphorus	117 mg
Iron	6.0 mg
Sodium	16 mg
Potassium	950 mg

STONE FRUITS

Almonds, apricots, cherries, nectarines, peaches, and plums are called stone fruits because their fruits are drupes that have thin outer skins (with the exception of the almond) encasing soft, juicy fruit and a stone-like pit surrounding the large seed. Stone fruits are species of the genus Prunus, members of the subfamily Prunoideae (Amygdaloideae) within the Rosaceae family.

of variety or cultivar. You can judge a ripe — or potenially ripe — peach or nectarine by the background color. The background of a ripe fruit will never be tinged with green, which means the fruit was picked when immature, before the sugar content was high enough to trigger ripening. Such fruits will have no aroma and grow soft without developing sweet, juicy, flavorful flesh. Also avoid over-mature fruit that is heavily bruised. Those with bruises should be used immediately in shakes, purées, sauces, pancakes, and waffles, for example.

A ripe peach or nectarine will feel heavy and smell tantalizingly aromatic — a good reason to smell the fruits before you buy. Select fruits that yield to light pressure and are free of soft spots and wrinkled skin. To soften firm-ripe fruits (hard, immature fruits will never ripen), place them in a single layer in a paper bag and fold over the top — this will trap the gases and speed the softening

process. Leave the fruits at room temperature for two to three days, until they yield slightly to the touch and deliver a sweet aroma. They can also be refrigerated for two to three days.

When you bring home a few pounds of soft-ripe peaches and nectarines, those that won't be eaten immediately should be placed — unwashed — in a single layer in a paper bag and refrigerated for two days. (Do not refrigerate in plastic bags; any condensation produced by the moist flesh will cause the fruits to rot.) To enjoy the full flavor and aroma, bring the fruits to room temperature before eating.

If you go to a pick-your-own orchard and lug back a large basket of ripe, juicy peaches and nectarines, you're bound to find a few bruised fruits in the mix. When the skin is broken or the flesh damaged, these soft fruits deteriorate quickly and will spread rot and mold to unblemished ones. Separate them as soon as you get home, refrigerate the unblemished, and use the bruised fruits the same day.

Apricots *(Prunus armeniaca)*

The apricot is an oval-shaped, egg-sized fruit with golden orange skin that is sometimes blushed with pink. When allowed to ripen on the tree, apricots become quite juicy. Unlike the other stone fruits, apricot kernels are edible and sweet and, like almonds, can be crushed to create oil for flavoring baked goods.

The name *apricot* translates from the Latin *praecox*, meaning precocious, because it grows early in the spring. The apricot can be traced to the Russian border and the Great Wall region of northern China, where the Chinese cultivated these fruit-bearing trees 3,000 to 4,000 years ago. Apricots spread through central Asia to the Middle East and northern Africa. Alexander the Great brought apricot cuttings from Persia to Greece, and the Romans transported the fruits to Italy in 70 to 60 BCE. The fruits proliferated in Mediterranean countries, where their delicate blossoms were in no danger of damage by late frosts. Apricots weren't planted in Britain until the 13th century. They were first introduced by Spanish missionaries to California in the 1770s.

Unfortunately, because apricots are such tender fruits, when fully ripe they bruise easily and quickly deteriorate. In the first century BCE, Pliny remarked, "There is no other fruit which keeps worse." For this reason, commercially grown apricots are harvested when hard so they will resist the rigors of transportation.

Indeed, the apricot varieties that are shipped out of state are grown not for their sweet, complex flavors but for their sturdy flesh. Though apricots are grown in 35 states, California cultivates more than 90 percent of the U.S. market, beginning the harvest in May. Other states of commercial importance are Washington, Utah, and Texas. Apricots do not grow well in the Northeast. Besides the United States, apricot-growing countries include Chile, New Zealand, and many Middle Eastern and Mediterranean nations.

Selecting and Storing

Tree-ripened fresh apricots are superb, but it's not easy to find them. Apricots that are to be shipped for fresh consumption are picked firm-mature because once they start to ripen on trees, they become too soft for transporting. Even firm-mature apricots have a short, one-week shelf life when held at 32°F. For this reason, the bulk of the harvest is dried, canned, or frozen; only 20 percent is destined for the fresh market.

If you live in a region where you are near a local source of tree-ripened apricots, rejoice at the chance to buy them. When truly ripe, they exude a wonderful aroma and taste lusciously sweet.

Select those that are fragrantly aromatic with velvety smooth skin and uniform golden to yellow-orange color. Ripe apricots will be plump, and their flesh should yield to gentle pressure. Avoid those with a green undertone. This is an indication of immature fruits that will remain hard, flavorless, and lacking in sweetness.

If all you can find are hard apricots, place them in a paper bag at room temperature, away from sun and other forms of heat, until they turn a rich yellow and soften, about three days.

Avoid storing ripe or softened apricots at room temperature because they will dry out and become mealy. When you're lucky enough to find juicy ripe apricots and buy a few pounds (there are 8 to 12 apricots in one pound), plan on using them within two days. If there are too many to use immediately, place the ripe fruits in a single layer in a paper bag

APRICOTS
USDA Dietary Values per 100 grams raw edible portion (3 medium-sized apricots)

Water	85.3 percent
Calories	51
Protein	1 g
Fat	0.2 g
Carbohydrates	12.8 g
Fiber	0.6 g
Vitamin A	2,770 IU (International Units)
Thiamin, B_1	0.03 mg
Riboflavin, B_2	0.04 mg
Niacin	0.6 mg
Vitamin C	10 mg
Calcium	17 mg
Phosphorus	23 mg
Iron	0.5 mg
Sodium	1 mg
Potassium	281 mg

DRIED APRICOTS
USDA Dietary Values per 100 grams uncooked dried apricots (about ¾ cup). Dried apricots contain more concentrated nutrients than fresh apricots.

Water	25%
Calories	260
Protein	5 g
Fat	0.5 g
Carbohydrates	66.5 g
Fiber	3 g
Vitamin A	10,900 IU (International Units)
Thiamin, B_1	0.01 mg
Riboflavin, B_2	0.16 mg
Niacin	3.3 mg
Vitamin C	12 mg
Calcium	67 mg
Phosphorus	108 mg
Iron	5.5 mg
Sodium	26 mg
Potassium	979 mg

and store in the refrigerator in a bin or drawer for one day. If they are firm-ripe, they can be stored in a perforated plastic bag for one to two days.

Don't wash the fruits until you are ready to use them and, for the best flavor, allow them to come to room temperature before eating. Apricots have thin, smooth, tender skin, so it's not necessary to peel them. Simply slice them in two along the seam or gently separate the halves with your fingers and pluck out the stone. Handle ripe apricots gently to avoid damaging the skin.

After the wonderful experience of eating ripe apricots out of hand, turn extras into any of the sweet or savory recipes sprinkled throughout this book. They can be used in many recipes that call

DRYING APRICOTS

Apricots grown for the dried market are harvested when they are fully ripe. In the United States, they are halved and pitted — either by machine or manually — and placed cut-side up on drying trays. At this point, they may be dried in sun-drenched dry yards or in large dehydrators.

Depending on temperature and humidity, those that are sun dried will remain in the dry yard for one day to one week before being moved into the shade to complete the curing process. Most dried apricots are treated with sulfur dioxide to preserve nutrients, flavor, and bright color.

for nectarines or peaches. Because fresh apricots are not around for long, canned apricots may be substituted in many dishes.

Plums

Like nectarines, all plum varieties have smooth skin and firm flesh that surrounds a stone, but there the similarity ends. There are more variations within the plum family than within just about any other fruit. For one thing, plums come in a wide range of colors with which no other fruits can compare — their flesh and their skins span the spectrum. There are plums with red, blue, purple, yellow, amber, translucent gold, pale green, and white flesh. Their skins are even more striking in blue-black, light purple, purple-black, pink, red, burgundy, yellow, lemon, gold, light green, dark green, and even mottled. Plums also differ widely in size, shape, aroma, flavor, sugar content, and firmness of flesh.

There are several major classes of plums grown throughout the world, the best known of which are in the *Euprunus* group of "true plums." These include European, Greengage, Damson, and Japanese. Hybrid cultivars of these true plums also include new specialty fruits: apriums, pluots, and plumcots, which are crosses between plums and apricots.

Another important group, known as *Prunocerasus* or "cherry plums," includes the

The New Specialty Hybrids

We want our apricots, nectarines, peaches, and plums to be juicy and candy-sweet or tangy-sweet. That's why breeders are working hard to develop new varieties. Some of the specialty hybrids that are becoming increasingly available in the supermarkets are crosses between apricots and plums or plums and peaches.

Pluot. This hybrid is 70 percent plum, 30 percent apricot. It looks and tastes like incredibly sweet and juicy plums without the tart skin.

Plumcot. This is 50 percent apricot, 50 percent plum. It resembles a large yellow-orange apricot with the flavor of a sweet, ripe plum.

Aprium. This fruit is 75 percent apricot, 25 percent plum. It's an apricot down to the pit except for the mild plum flavor. To date, they are marketed commercially as apricots.

Plantings of these specialty hybrids represented 20 percent of California's plum market in 2002, with pluots taking the lion's share at 10 percent. The state's marketing board has already forecasted that their share of the market will increase to 50 percent by 2010. Pluot varieties are such a success story because the dominant plum gene gives them a longer shelf life than those ruled by apricot parentage. While shelf life is a consideration for growers, distributors, and supermarkets, however, consumers are more delighted that the pluot is plump and firm yet tender and lusciously juicy and that its honey-sweet flesh is balanced with a touch of tanginess but not the tart flavor so characteristic of many plum varieties. With its shiny, smooth skin, the pluot resembles a plum in appearance. Pluots come in a range of colors and, depending on variety, may be black, purple, red, yellow, pink mottled with green, or other variations.

The half-plum, half-apricot parentage of plumcots has produced some successful varieties that are striking in appearance as well as in taste. Currently, the main plumcot produced in California is the Flavorella. Not only does it ship well, but it has the appearance of a golden yellow apricot and the wonderful sweet-tart flavor of a ripe, juicy plum. One of the most striking plumcots is the Eden Pride, grown by Steve Brenkwitz of Eden Garden. (See the Brenkwitz Family profile on page 14.) This plumcot was an experimental cross developed by Zaiger Nursery in Modesto, California. The unnamed hybrid was considered difficult, if not impossible, to fruit. Brenkwitz, however, managed to grow a show-stopper: Eden Pride is a large, bright orange and tantalizingly aromatic plumcot with juicy, syrupy-sweet flesh that tastes of plum.

Apriums are three-quarter apricot, so it's not surprising that they resemble that side of their heritage much more than their plum connection. While they do have a distinctive sweet flavor tinged with plum, and their flesh can have a translucent plum quality, they are apricot look-alikes with yellow-orange skin and golden yellow flesh.

Peacotums are large, round, experimental peach-apricot-plum crosses, with rosy red skin and yellow flesh. These and other experimental crosses, including white apricots and Nectaplums, are earmarked for release around 2010.

A white peach-plum named Snow Peach is already being marketed as a white peach by California growers. Also available are new varieties of low-acid white- and yellow-fleshed peaches and nectarines. Low-acid fruits like Sweet Scarlet peaches and Honey Kist and Arctic Rose nectarines are deliciously sweet and juicy when picked firm. (See Peaches and Nectarines on page 2 for more information.)

All of these specialty stone fruits have been developed and patented during the last 40 years by breeder Floyd Zaiger, of the Zaiger Nursery in California. Zaiger started developing these crosses in the 1950s after working for Fred Anderson, a student of Luther Burbank who went on to breed the first sweet nectarine. Burbank, who was considered the greatest fruit breeder of his day, developed most of the Japanese plum varieties that are today's stalwarts of the industry. Burbank also introduced the first plum-apricot cross in 1911. Called the Apex plumcot, it has deep pink or crimson skin and honey-yellow flesh with some flavor. It was not a commercial success, however, and is now a classified California Rare Fruit, grown by collectors. Zaiger picked up where Burbank left off, and in 1989 he introduced his first patented plum-apricot cross, called the pluot.

Unlike traditional apricots, plums, and most older varieties of yellow peaches and nectarines, Zaiger's low-acid stone fruit hybrids break all standards. These varieties are sweet and juicy with good to exceptional flavor even when their flesh is crisp. This allows them to be picked and shipped when firm, which reduces the risk of bruising. The older, high-acid varieties require tree ripening in order to develop the satisfactory sugar level that gives them that wonderful syrupy juice and honey-sweet flavor. Unfortunately, once they are fully ripe, they have no shelf life and are no longer suitable for shipping.

PEACH AND NECTARINE EQUIVALENTS

If your recipe calls for 1 pound of peaches or nectarines, buy three or four medium-sized or two large ones. Nectarines tend to be smaller, so the best measurement is by weight. One pound of peaches or nectarines is roughly equivalent to 2 cups sliced, 1⅔ cups chopped, and 1½ cups purée.

native American wild plums, the most important of which are *Prunus americana, Prunus hortulana, Prunus munsoniana, Prunus nigra,* and the beach plum *Prunus maritime.* These native plums have proved invaluable in the breeding of European and Japanese hybrid cultivars.

REFRIGERATION HESITATION

For the best-tasting peaches, plums, and nectarines, don't refrigerate unless the fruit is overripe or soft-ripe and can't be eaten in a day or two. When hard-mature stone fruits — those that don't yield to pressure and have no aroma — are stored in cold temperatures below 50°F, they become mealy, dry, and tasteless. To allow the flesh to soften and become juicy and flavorful, hold them at a temperature no lower than 50°F — between 65 and 75°F is ideal. If they have already been subjected to too-cold temperatures during transportation from orchard to fruit supplier or from fruit supplier to supermarket, they will have already suffered from internal breakdown. That's why, unless they are the newer varieties that continue to ripen off the tree, so many peaches, plums, and nectarines are disappointing when they have been picked mature but not tree ripe and shipped from the southern hemisphere during the winter or long distance domestically early in the season.

Of the thousands of varieties of plums, more than 500 are cultivated worldwide. California leads plum production with more than 200 varieties — 90 percent of the plums produced in the United States are grown in the San Joaquin/Central Valley region. More than 35 percent of the California plum harvest is of the Santa Rosa variety; other varieties grown are Casselman, Elephant Heart, El Dorado, Greengage, and Laroda. Plums are also grown on a commercial scale in Washington, Oregon, Idaho, Michigan, and to a lesser extent New York. Outside of the United States, Chile is the dominant producer of both Japanese and European plum varieties. Other countries producing plums on a large scale are Argentina, South Africa, Germany, Turkey, and Japan.

Japanese Plums *(Prunus salicina)*

Japanese plums are large fruits that are oval to pointed and round to heart-shaped with sweet, juicy flesh. The flesh usually reflects the color of the skin, which may be golden, orange-red, red, or purple-black.

The Japanese plum originated in China more than 2,000 years ago, but only reached the shores of Japan in the early 16th century. From there, it was introduced to the rest of the world as the

Japanese plum. In 1870, fruit breeder Luther Burbank purchased a few Japanese plum trees to plant at his farm in Santa Rosa, California. Through crossbreeding, he was able to produce many modern plum varieties, including the Santa Rosa and the Satsuma. Japanese plums are commercially popular because they bear earlier, are more vigorous and disease resistant than others, and are able to tolerate warmer temperatures than European plums. They are also larger, firmer, and juicier and come in a wider range of colors than European plums.

European Plums *(Prunus domestica)*

European plums are smaller, firmer, and less juicy than the Japanese plums. The European prune plums, however, are much sweeter. According to Mark Rieger, professor of horticulture at the University of Georgia, fruit growers often divide the European plums into four classes: prune, greengage, damson, and Lombard.

PRUNE PLUMS

These oval, blue-purple, freestone cultivars have a high sugar content. The primary European plum variety grown in California for the dried market is Prune d'Agen, or the French prune. Benedictine monks returning from the Crusades in Persia in the 14th century introduced these plums into Europe, where they have since thrived.

European prune plums were introduced to America in 1856. Some of the main European prune plums are Prune d'Agen (or Petite d'Agen), Stanley, and Italian. Because prune plums are intensely sweet, they are commonly called "sugar plums" for the fresh market.

GREENGAGE PLUMS *(PRUNUS ITALICA)*

These are firm, medium-sized plums with greenish yellow or golden skin and flesh and a tangy sweet flavor. They are also known as gages. When tree ripe, these late-summer to early-autumn plums are aromatic, sweet, and juicy, and a treat to eat out of hand. When picked early at the firmhard stage, greengages are excellent for canning, freezing, and making into jam.

The greengage species was discovered in Asia Minor and introduced into northern Europe by the Romans. The species disappeared from cultivation in Europe during the Middle Ages and was not reintroduced until around 1725 in France. French varieties are the small yellow mirabelles (favorite plums with the canning industry) and the Reine Claude, with greenish yellow skin and pale flesh. It was the pale green Reine Claude plum that was the first of its kind to be brought into Britain by Sir Thomas Gage, who called them

THE BRENKWITZ FAMILY

Steve Brenkwitz is a fifth-generation stone fruit farmer whose family has been cultivating apricots since the mid-19th century. While proud to be continuing this family tradition, Steve and his father, Thomas F. Brenkwitz, have also kept pace with 20th-century demands by embracing the new apricot-plum hybrids. During the last 10 years, they have also been growing apriums, plumcots, and pluots at Eden Garden, the 200-acre family farm located in the San Joaquin Valley, California.

Steve's great-great-grandfather Frank Wrede started the farm in the 1860s, not long after arriving from Germany. Taking advantage of the sheltered, fertile location, Wrede planted one of the first apricot orchards, in Hayward, near the southern tip of the Santa Clara Valley. Sixty years later, the region was planted over with so many apricot, peach, plum, and cherry trees that it was called the Valley of Heart's Delight. However, with the growth of the computer industry in the 1950s, business and residential developments replaced agricultural land and this valley of flowering fruit trees gave way to Silicon Valley.

Feeling the squeeze of urban sprawl during the mid-60s, Thomas F. Brenkwitz relocated Eden Garden's apricot operation to Tracy, in the southern region of the San Joaquin Valley, and planted new varieties of apricots along with the older ones that patriarch Frank Wrede and Steve's grandpa Thomas N. Brenkwitz had favored. "Grandpa was an awesome figure in our lives and he's the reason why we continue to expand and improve Eden Garden," said Steve. By the mid-1990s, the Brenkwitz family had also started to grow experimental plum-apricot crosses developed by Floyd Zaiger, of Modesto, California. (See The New Specialty Hybrid, page 10.)

Today, the Brenkwitz family cultivates and ships more than 40 varieties of apricots, pluots, and plumcots, and a few experimental apriums. The family is constantly researching and developing new varieties to expand production of the most desirable fruits, often experimenting with 50 varieties to come up with one good one. "Our goal is to grow fruits that taste as good as they look regardless of their fragility," says Steve. "We want to be assured that they arrive at your door in perfect condition." With this in mind, Eden Garden continues to refine its packing and shipping techniques so that these tender fruits are not bruised during transportation — whether it's sending one box to individuals who mail-order through its Web site or sending large shipments to commercial clients in the North America, Asia, and Europe.

Whether they are old or new varieties, all stone fruits have tender skin and flesh that bruises easily. This means they must be harvested by hand. The older varieties of apricots are especially fragile, particularly the luscious Blenheim, a favorite of anyone who loves apricots. "Take one bite into a Blenheim and you will then know what a real apricot tastes like," says Steve. "The flesh is sweet and tart and meltingly juicy."

In spite of their sublime flavor and soft, velvety flesh, most commercial growers have stopped growing Blenheims because they're not perfectly shaped, they don't ship well, and they have a short shelf life. Produce wholesalers and supermarkets shun this old-fashioned variety in favor of the firm-fleshed and less flavorful Castlebrite and Patterson, which account for 50 percent of California's apricot crop.

Brenkwitz also grows Patterson apricots because there is a big market for them. Like Castlebrite, they are large, well shaped, have good color, and their firm texture ensures a shelf life of a week or longer. And even though they are not an apricot you'd gobble out of hand straight from the supermarket, they will ripen in storage. Cooking develops their flavor and softens their texture, making them a favorite for processing and canning. According to Steve, "Patterson is a very good cot when left to tree ripeness. Problem is they keep picking it more and more immature."

Like many other growers, Steve Brenkwitz continues to develop and test new apricot varieties that will please both consumers and marketers. One apricot that is bound to be a big hit is named for his wife, Mary Anne. "This is a large apricot with a beautiful crimson blush splashed over golden skin," says Steve. "The texture is firmer and crisper than the Blenheim's, but the flavor is sweet and strong."

Apriums, pluots, and plumcots are challenging fruits to grow and harvest because, even though they are not as fragile as traditional apricots, they have thin, tender skin that bruises easily when overhandled. They occupy 30 percent of the Eden Garden orchards, however, because they are intensely flavorful and bursting with juice and sugar. "These new fruits have a bright future because they are so incredibly sweet and so delicious to eat fresh," Steve says. There's Flavor Heart, for example, a beautiful black pluot with greenish yellow flesh. This pluot is so sweet it measures 24 on the Brix scale, putting it right up there with the sweetest peaches and nectarines. Brenkwitz also likes the tarter Flavor King, which he says are a special treat when cooked down with sugar into a sauce for spooning over ice cream.

The Brenkwitz family never tire of the fruit they grow, eating them daily when in season — out of hand and in pies, tarts, cakes, and many other recipes prepared by Mary Anne. Says Steve, "With all the hard work that goes into growing stone fruits, you have to like what you're doing and enjoy eating what you grow."

Gage plums. Hence, the name greengage became the accepted horticultureal designation for *Prunus italica*. Reine Claude is now considered a variety of greengage. Hybrid gages have been produced from crosses with European plums.

DAMSONS (*PRUNUS INSTITIA*)

The damson bears small, oval fruits with blue-black skin and amber flesh that offers a taste-tingling experience of a tartly sweet and spicy flavor. Damsons originated in or near Damascus and were brought to Europe in the 12th century during the Crusades. These are the wild plums of Europe, which were cultivated before the introduction of European plums and then used as rootstocks. Because these small plums are tart and high in pectin — plus they are a chore to pit — they are used primarily for making into jams and jellies.

LOMBARD PLUMS

These large, oval, red or pink plums include the Victoria and Lombard cultivars, which are so popular in Europe. The Victoria is a prime commercial plum because it predictably produces bounteous harvests of plump, pinkish purple fruits with sweet, juicy flesh. However, because it lacks tartness, it does not have great flavor and is favored for canning and cooking rather than fresh eating.

Cherry Plums (*Prunus cerasifera*) and Native Species

The cherry or myrobalan plums are yellow, red, or purple. They are small and oval, like damsons, but sweeter and juicier. These plums originated in the Balkans, Caucasus, and western Asia. They were introduced into Britain in the 16th century and brought to North America in the 17th century by English settlers. By interbreeding the cherry plum with native American species — wild chickasaw and beach plums — they developed crosses that were hardier and could withstand the harsh American winters.

Long before the arrival of the European settlers, Native Americans had been cultivating and harvesting small, tart wild plums. Today, the chickasaw hybrids grown on the rootstocks of the cherry plum are sweeter and larger than the original sour wild plums. The native American plum cultivars are used mostly for making jams, jellies, and sauces. They have also become popular with gardeners favoring native plantings — especially those ornamental forms bearing pink flowers and purple leaves.

Beach plums are seldom cultivated and still grow wild along the Atlantic seaboard from Canada to Virginia. Too sour to eat raw when ripe, these little blue-purple plums offer a superb flavor when made into jams and jellies with plenty of sweetener.

Dried Plums

USDA Dietary Values per 100 grams uncooked dried plums (about ½ cup). Dried plums (prunes) contain more concentrated nutrients than fresh.

Water	28 percent
Calories	255
Protein	2.1 g
Fat	0.6 g
Carbohydrates	67.4 g
Fiber	1.6 g
Vitamin A	1,600 IU (International Units)
Thiamin, B_1	0.09 mg
Riboflavin, B_2	0.17 mg
Niacin	1.6 mg
Vitamin C	3 mg
Calcium	51 mg
Phosphorus	79 mg
Iron	3.9 mg
Sodium	8 mg
Potassium	694 mg

Plums

USDA Dietary Values per 100 grams raw edible portion (about 2 medium-sized Japanese plums or pluots).

The equivalent weight of damsons and greengages provides approximately the same dietary values, except slightly higher vitamin A content. Italian prune plums are four times higher in vitamin A.

Water	86.6 percent
Calories	48
Protein	0.5 g
Fat	0.2 g
Carbohydrates	12.3 g
Fiber	0.6 g
Vitamin A	250 IU (International Units)
Thiamin, B_1	0.03 mg
Riboflavin, B_2	0.03 mg
Niacin	0.05 mg
Vitamin C	6 mg
Calcium	12 mg
Phosphorus	18 mg
Iron	0.5 mg
Sodium	1 mg
Potassium	170 mg

Selecting and Storing

The Santa Rosa, one of the most popular plums with consumers anywhere and one of the favorites at farmers' markets in California, may be one of the only plums recognizable by name in the supermarkets. Retailers tend to label plums as "California red plums," "California black plums," or simply "tree ripe" or "local."

The first domestic plums are available from California in May, with the rest of the country also producing harvests from July through September. California plums are available through Thanksgiving.

It's not always easy to choose a ripe plum based on color; the varieties develop good color before they're mature so that a hard, unripe plum could be as deep a purple or as bright a red or yellow as those that are firm-mature or firm-ripe.

One of the best ways to recognize ripe plums (as well as pluots, plumcots, apricots, apriums, peaches, and nectarines) is by sniffing for the sweet, sometimes spicy, aroma that is obvious as soon as you pick one up. At that time you will also feel the flesh give a little and will appreciate the heaviness that is associated with generous sugar and juice content. Select plump plums with smooth, tender skin.

Avoid rock-hard plums, the sign of immature fruits, which will be more sour than tart. Avoid plums that are very soft to the touch or have shriveled, bruised, or broken skin. Don't worry about those that are somewhat dull with a whitish haze; this is a natural "bloom" and indicates that they have not been overhandled.

Very soft fruits are not good for eating out of hand. However, if they are not showing brown spots, overripe plums (like overripe peaches and nectarines) can be used in shakes, sauces, purées, soups, and other dishes in which texture and shape are not an issue.

Commercial plums are usually picked mature but not fully ripe to ensure that they are sufficiently firm to withstand transportation. Plums that are picked at this stage will ripen within a day or two at room temperature (between 55 and 75°F), during which time they will become softer and develop a sweet or spicy aroma. To accelerate the ripening process, place them in a paper bag with an ethylene-producing fruit such as apple, banana, or pear.

Ripe fruit may be refrigerated in a vegetable bin for up to three days in a perforated plastic bag. To prevent them from sweating, place a paper towel in the plastic bag and lay the plums on top in a single layer. Don't store ripe plums with apples, bananas, or pears.

BREAKFASTS AND BREADS

Peaches and nectarines are old favorites for adding flavor and moisture to quick breads, muffins, pancakes, waffles, or other breakfast dishes and baked treats. Plums and apricots are also easy to include in or alongside anything sweet or savory. You'll find plenty of ideas in this chapter for starting out or ending the day with these luscious, colorful fruits.

Dried Plum—Banana Bread

MAKES 12 SERVINGS

Substitute dried apricots for the dried plums and cinnamon for the cardamom and you'll get totally different flavors. The dried plums make this a sweet, dense bread, so you may prefer to increase the sugar by ¼ cup if using dried apricots.

1. Preheat the oven to 350°F. Spray an 8- by 4-inch loaf pan with cooking oil spray.
2. Mix the flour, baking powder, baking soda, cardamom, and nutmeg in a large mixing bowl. Make a well in the center.
3. Mash the bananas in a medium-sized bowl and beat in the sugar, oil, and eggs. Pour into the center of the dry ingredients and stir until just mixed.
4. Stir the plums into the batter.
5. Spoon the batter into the loaf pan and bake for about 1 hour, or until a toothpick inserted in the center comes out clean. Cool in the pan for 10 minutes. Remove the loaf and cool completely on a wire rack.

Cooking oil spray

1¾ cups sifted all-purpose flour

2 teaspoons baking powder

½ teaspoon baking soda

½ teaspoon ground cardamom

½ teaspoon ground nutmeg

2 ripe medium-sized bananas, mashed (about 1 cup)

½ cup firmly packed brown sugar

⅓ cup canola or olive oil

2 eggs or ½ cup egg substitute

8 ounces pitted dried plums, quartered

Apricot-Apple-Nut Bread

Cooking oil spray

1 cup mashed ripe apricots
(¾ pound fresh or a 15-ounce
can, drained)

¾ cup sugar

¼ cup butter, softened

2 eggs or ½ cup egg substitute

Zest of about ½ orange
or ⅔ lemon (2 teaspoons)

2 cups presifted all-purpose
flour

1 teaspoon baking powder

1 teaspoon baking soda

¼ teaspoon ground cardamom
or allspice

1 large apple (Braeburn,
Jonagold, Fuji work well),
cored and chopped

¾ cup chopped hazelnuts
or walnuts

*Substitute fresh peaches or plums
when they are at their peak.*

1. Preheat the oven to 350°F. Spray an 8- by 4-inch loaf pan with cooking oil spray.
2. Place the apricots, sugar, butter, eggs, and zest in a large bowl and whip together with an electric beater.
3. Stir in the flour, baking powder, baking soda, and cardamom until mixed. Fold in the chopped apple and hazelnuts.
4. Spoon the batter into the pan and bake for 1 hour, or until a toothpick inserted in the center comes out clean. Cool for 10 minutes in the pan, remove, and cool completely on a wire rack.

FRUITED BREADS AND MUFFINS

Whether you mash, purée, dice, or slice them, don't hesitate to add 1 cup of peaches or other juicy fruits to muffins and quick breads. They will add moisture as well as nutrition. If a recipe calls for ripe bananas and yours are green, substitute the same quantity of mashed or puréed peaches, apricots, or plums. Even in the depths of winter, you probably have a can of one or another just waiting to be used. Adding dried fruits like apricots and plums (dried plums are what used to be exclusively known as prunes) also adds nuggets of intense flavors.

Dried Peach and Sunflower Seed Quick Bread

MAKES 12 SERVINGS

Dried peaches are surprisingly moist and chewy and are good additions to quick breads and muffins.

1. Preheat the oven to 350°F. Spray a 9- by 5-inch loaf pan with cooking oil spray.
2. Mix the whole wheat flour, wheat germ, allspice, baking powder, and baking soda in a large bowl. Make a well in the center.
3. Beat together the honey, yogurt, apple juice, oil, and eggs in a small bowl. Pour into the center of the dry ingredients and stir until just moistened. Stir in the peaches and sunflower seeds.
4. Spoon the batter into the prepared loaf pan and bake in the oven for 50 to 55 minutes, or until a toothpick inserted in the center comes out clean. Cool in the pan on a wire rack for 10 minutes. Remove from the pan and cool completely on a wire rack.

Cooking oil spray

1¾ cups whole wheat flour

½ cup wheat germ

2 teaspoons ground allspice

2 teaspoons baking powder

1 teaspoon baking soda

½ cup honey

8 ounces peach or vanilla nonfat yogurt

½ cup apple juice or green tea

¼ cup canola or olive oil

2 eggs or ½ cup egg substitute

1 cup chopped dried peaches

1 cup sunflower seeds

Peach-Jalapeño Corn Bread

MAKES 12 SERVINGS

Jalapeños are mildly hot but the little bit of heat goes well with the fruit. Use this recipe for Apricot-Pecan Corn Bread Stuffing on page 85.

Cooking oil spray

1 cup yellow cornmeal

1 cup all-purpose flour

3 tablespoons sugar

1 tablespoon baking powder

1 teaspoon baking soda

¼ teaspoon salt (or to taste)

½ cup low-fat sour cream

¼ cup low-fat milk

¼ cup olive or canola oil

1 egg or ¼ cup egg substitute

2 medium-sized peaches or nectarines, pitted and diced (about 1⅓ cups)

2 red or green jalapeño peppers, seeded and diced (about ⅓ cup)

1. Preheat the oven to 400°F. Spray an 8-inch square baking pan with cooking oil spray.
2. Mix the cornmeal, flour, sugar, baking powder, baking soda, and salt in a large bowl. Make a well in the center.
3. Beat together the sour cream, milk, oil, and egg in a small bowl. Stir in the chopped peaches and jalapeños and pour into the dry ingredients. Stir until just evenly moistened.
4. Spoon the batter into the prepared pan and bake for 25 to 30 minutes, or until a toothpick inserted in the center comes out clean. Allow to cool in the pan; serve warm.

Blueberry-Apricot Cornmeal Muffins

These colorful muffins are also delightful when made into one-bite (almost) gems — use thirty-six 1¾-inch muffin cups and bake in a 400°F oven for 15 minutes. If desired, add 2 teaspoons of lemon zest to the batter.

1. Preheat the oven to 425°F. Spray a 12-cup muffin pan or 36-cup "gem" pan with cooking oil spray or line with paper liners.
2. Mix the cornmeal, flour, sugar, baking powder, baking soda, and nutmeg in a large bowl. Make a well in the center.
3. Beat together the milk, oil, and eggs. Pour into the dry ingredients and stir until just evenly moistened.
4. Fold in the apricots and blueberries.
5. Spoon the batter into the muffin cups and bake for 20 minutes, or until a toothpick inserted in the center comes out clean.

Cooking oil spray
or muffin liners

1 cup yellow cornmeal

1 cup all-purpose flour

½ cup sugar

1 tablespoon baking powder

½ teaspoon baking soda

½ teaspoon ground nutmeg

¾ cup low-fat or nonfat milk

⅓ cup olive or canola oil
or melted butter

2 eggs or ½ cup egg substitute

1 cup chopped dried apricots

1 cup fresh or frozen
blueberries

Plum Jam and Black Walnut Muffins

Cooking oil spray
or muffin liners

2½ cups sifted all-purpose
flour

½ cup sugar

1 tablespoon baking powder

1 teaspoon ground nutmeg

1 cup chopped black walnuts

1 cup low-fat or nonfat milk
(or substitute soy- or rice milk)

⅓ cup olive or canola oil
or melted butter

2 eggs or ½ cup egg substitute

½ cup Plum Jam
(see page 48)

Substitute English walnuts or pecans if you are not a black walnut aficionado. The flavor of black walnuts complements the Plum Jam.

1. Preheat the oven to 425°F and spray 12 muffin cups with cooking oil spray or line them with paper liners.
2. Mix the flour, sugar, baking powder, nutmeg, and walnuts in a large bowl. Make a well in the center.
3. Beat together the milk, oil, and eggs in a small bowl. Pour into the dry ingredients and stir until just mixed.
4. Spoon half of the batter into the muffin cups. Center 2 teaspoons of the jam on top of each half-filled cup and cover with the remaining batter.
5. Bake for 20 minutes, or until a toothpick inserted in the center comes out clean.

Honey-Apricot-Almond Muffins

Fresh, canned, or frozen (and thawed) plums or peaches are also good choices. To toast the almonds, cook for 3 minutes in a dry 9-inch skillet over medium heat, stirring occasionally to keep the nuts from burning. If desired, substitute pecans for the almonds — no need to toast pecans because they already have such a lovely nutty flavor.

1. Preheat the oven to 425°F. Spray a 12-cup muffin pan with cooking oil spray or line with paper liners.
2. Mix the almonds, flour, oats, baking powder, ginger, baking soda, and salt in a large bowl. Make a well in the center.
3. Beat together the honey, yogurt, milk, oil, and eggs in a small bowl. Stir in the apricots. Pour into the dry ingredients and stir until just mixed and evenly moistened.
4. Spoon the batter into the muffin cups and bake for 20 to 25 minutes, or until a toothpick inserted in the center comes out clean.

Cooking oil spray
or muffin liners

1 cup flaked almonds

1 cup sifted all-purpose flour

1 cup quick rolled oats
(not instant)

1 tablespoon baking powder

1 teaspoon ground ginger

½ teaspoon baking soda

¼ teaspoon salt

1 cup honey

1 cup nonfat apricot
or peach yogurt

¼ cup low-fat milk

¼ cup olive or canola oil
or melted butter

2 eggs or ½ cup egg substitute

1 pound ripe apricots, pitted and chopped, or 1 can (16 ounces) apricots in juice or light syrup (if desired, substitute the drained juice for the milk)

Double Plum and Orange Muffins

Delicious cold, these orange-flavored muffins are divine when warm.

Cooking oil spray
or muffin liners

1½ cups all-purpose flour

½ cup whole wheat flour

1 teaspoon baking powder

1 teaspoon baking soda

½ cup buttermilk
or low-fat milk

½ cup honey

¼ cup olive or canola oil
or melted butter

2 eggs or ½ cup egg substitute

Juice and zest of 1 medium
orange (about ⅓ cup juice
and 1 teaspoon zest)

2 large red plums,
pitted and diced

1 cup orange-flavored pitted
dried plums, sliced

3 tablespoons light
brown sugar

1. Preheat the oven to 425°F. Spray a 12-cup muffin pan with cooking oil spray or line with paper liners.
2. Mix the flours, baking powder, and baking soda in a large bowl. Make a well in the center.
3. Beat together the buttermilk, honey, oil, eggs, orange juice, and zest. Stir in the fresh plums.
4. Pour the liquid mixture into the center of the dry ingredients and mix until just evenly moist. Fold in the dried plums.
5. Spoon the batter into the muffin cups and sprinkle ½ teaspoon of the sugar over the top of each. Bake for 20 minutes, or until a toothpick inserted in the center comes out clean. Cool the muffins in the pan on a wire rack for 5 minutes. Remove and serve warm.

DRIED PLUMS AND APRICOTS

Today, most of the packaged dried plums and apricots we buy are plump and moist. If they are not (or your package was opened or not sealed properly), after cutting them in halves or quarters, cover with ½ cup of boiling water flavored with 1 tea bag of raspberry, lemon, jasmine, green, Earl Grey, or another favorite — true teas (not herbals) provide flavonoids as well as flavor, and the dried fruits will plump up with the liquid they absorb.

Cinnamon Prune Scones

At 95, my mother is still baking pies, cakes, and scones and making jams and chutneys from homegrown fruits and vegetables. She loves this recipe because it's easy to freeze. Arrange cooled scones in a single layer in gallon freezer bags with self-locking tops. For the best results, freeze no longer than 1 month. To thaw and reheat, preheat the oven to 300°F, wrap the frozen scones in foil, and warm for 20 to 25 minutes.

Cooking oil spray

2 cups sifted all-purpose flour

¼ cup sugar

½ teaspoon baking powder

½ teaspoon baking soda

½ teaspoon ground cinnamon

½ teaspoon ground ginger or nutmeg

¼ teaspoon salt

¼ cup butter, plus more for spreading

½ cup snipped dried plums (prunes) or dried apricots

¼ cup low-fat milk (use heavy cream for a richer dough)

1 egg, beaten, or ¼ cup egg substitute

Raspberry jam to spread on the scones (optional)

1. Preheat the oven to 425°F and lightly grease a baking tray or spray with cooking oil spray.
2. Mix the flour, sugar, baking powder, baking soda, cinnamon, ginger, and salt in a large bowl.
3. Cut in the butter with a pastry blender until the mixture resembles large crumbs. Make a well in the center.
4. Mix the plums, milk, and egg in a small bowl and pour into the dry ingredients. Stir with a fork until the dough clings together.
5. Lightly flour a cutting board. Pat the dough into a ½-inch-thick square on the board and cut the square into eight triangles, rounds, or squares.
6. Place on the prepared baking sheet and bake 10 to 12 minutes. (Alternatively, pat the dough into a 9-inch circle, place on the baking sheet, score the top into triangles, and bake 15 minutes.)
7. Use within 2 days or freeze. Split and spread with the butter and raspberry jam. Serve warm.

Filled Dried Plum and Nut Buns

Cooking oil spray

1 package (16 ounces) hot roll yeast mix (contains 1 packet yeast)

1 cup hot water

2 tablespoons canola oil or butter, softened

1 egg or ¼ cup egg substitute

1 cup pitted dried plums (prunes), diced

1 cup cold water

½ cup honey

Juice and zest of 1 lemon (about 3 tablespoons juice and 1 tablespoon zest)

1 cup chopped walnuts (black or English)

Confectioners' sugar for sprinkling (optional)

Make two of these for a brunch gathering. This is an easy way to make a special breakfast treat, but it will be even easier if you have a bread machine to work the flour mixture to the dough stage.

1. Prepare the hot roll mix with the hot water, oil, and egg according to the package directions.
2. While the dough is rising, bring to a boil the plums, cold water, honey, and lemon juice and zest in a saucepan over medium-high heat. Reduce the heat to low and cook for 10 minutes, until the mixture thickens.
3. Stir in the nuts, remove from the heat, and cool.
4. Punch down the dough and roll out on a lightly floured cutting board to form a 12- by 10-inch rectangle. Spread the dough with the plum and nut filling and roll up, beginning at the long side. Seal the edge tightly and cut into 12 slices, each 1 inch thick.
5. Preheat the oven to 375°F and spray a 12-cup muffin pan with cooking oil spray.
6. Place the slices in the prepared muffin pan. Cover and let rise in a warm place for 20 minutes or until doubled in size. Uncover the buns, place in the oven, and bake for 20 minutes, or until they are golden brown.
7. Set the muffin pan on a wire rack to cool. While hot, sprinkle with confectioners' sugar (if using).

Fruit Pancakes

Makes about 16 pancakes

1 cup low-fat or nonfat milk (or substitute soy- or rice milk)

1 cup chopped peaches, nectarines, or plums

½ cup all-purpose flour

½ cup whole wheat flour

1 tablespoon melted butter or canola oil

2 eggs, beaten, or ½ cup egg substitute

1 tablespoon canola oil or nonfat cooking spray

Fresh peach purée for topping

1. Stir the milk, peaches, flours, butter, and eggs together in a large bowl.
2. Heat ½ tablespoon of the oil in a large skillet and drop in large spoonfuls of the batter.
3. Cook over medium heat for about 2 minutes on each side, until golden brown.
4. Repeat with the remaining oil and batter. Serve hot with the peach purée.

Peach Waffles

Makes about 8 waffles

1½ cups all-purpose flour

¼ cup sugar

1 teaspoon baking powder

½ teaspoon baking soda

1 carton (8 ounces) nonfat peach yogurt

¾ cup low-fat buttermilk (or substitute soy milk or rice milk)

2 eggs or ½ cup egg substitute

2 tablespoons canola or olive oil or melted butter

1 ripe peach, pitted and mashed

Cooking oil spray

1. Mix the flour, sugar, baking powder, and baking soda in a medium-sized mixing bowl.
2. Beat the yogurt, buttermilk, eggs, and oil together in a small bowl until frothy. Stir in the mashed peach. Pour into the dry ingredients and mix thoroughly.
3. Spoon the batter onto a hot waffle iron sprayed with cooking oil spray and bake until golden.
4. Serve with a simple fruit sauce such as the one on page 73.

Peach-Plum Popover Pancakes

¼ cup butter, softened

1 pound plums, peaches,
or nectarines, pitted and cut
into thin slices (about 2 cups)

¾ cup sugar

1¼ cups all-purpose flour

1¼ cups low-fat or nonfat
milk

2 eggs or ½ cup egg substitute

2 teaspoons baking powder

*This giant fruit-filled popover pancake is a great
brunch dish to serve for family or friends.*

1. Preheat the oven to 375°F. Put the butter in a deep 2- to 3-quart casserole dish and place in the oven.
2. Toss the sliced fruits in a bowl with ¼ cup of the sugar.
3. Place the remaining ½ cup sugar and the flour, milk, eggs, and baking powder in a blender and liquify. Alternatively, place in a medium-sized bowl and work with an electric beater until the batter is smooth.
4. When the butter has melted to the sizzling point, 3 to 5 minutes, remove the hot dish from the oven. Immediately pour the batter into the dish and spoon the sugared fruit and any juice on top.
5. Return to the oven and bake for 50 minutes, or until the pancake has risen and is golden brown. Serve warm.

Baked French Toast with Fresh Fruit

MAKES 8 SERVINGS

This is another great dish to serve a large family or a few friends for brunch because you can prepare it the night before. This makes a double recipe, so split it in half for a family of three or four.

Cooking oil spray

3 eggs or ¾ cup egg substitute

1½ cups low-fat or nonfat milk (or substitute vanilla soy milk or rice milk)

1 tablespoon vanilla extract

1 teaspoon ground cinnamon

16 slices Italian bread cut ¾ inch thick

2 cups peach or apricot nectar

2 teaspoons cornstarch

2 cups sliced ripe apricots, peaches, nectarines, plums, or a combination

1. Spray two 9- by 13-inch baking dishes with cooking oil spray.
2. Place the eggs, milk, vanilla, and cinnamon in a blender and liquidize. Pour ½ cup of liquid into each baking dish and arrange eight slices of bread in each, pressing them together. Divide the remaining liquid in half and pour it evenly over the two dishes to cover all of the bread.
3. Cover with plastic wrap or foil and refrigerate for at least 2 and up to 12 hours.
4. When you're ready, preheat the oven to 350°F. Uncover the dishes and bake the French toast for 50 to 60 minutes, or until golden brown.
5. While the French toast is baking, combine the nectar with the cornstarch in a small saucepan and place over medium-high heat. Bring to a boil, stirring constantly; reduce the heat and simmer for 2 minutes. Remove from the heat, cool, and combine with the sliced fresh fruit. Serve on the side with the French toast.

Apricot-Peach Granola

MAKES 6½ CUPS

Cooking oil spray

4½ cups rolled oats

½ cup sliced almonds

½ cup sunflower seeds

½ cup wheat germ

½ cup honey

¼ cup apple juice

1 tablespoon ground cinnamon

1 tablespoon canola oil

1 tablespoon sesame oil

¾ cup chopped dried fruits (apricots, peaches, plums, or cherries)

My friend Annegrette Rice, an artist and yoga teacher, makes her own granola and brings it along when she comes to visit. I thought it was time I made some for her.

1. Preheat the oven to 350°F and lightly spray a baking sheet with cooking oil spray.
2. Mix the oats, almonds, sunflower seeds, and wheat germ in a large bowl.
3. Whisk together the honey, apple juice, cinnamon, and oils in a pitcher and pour into the oat mixture. Stir together until the dry ingredients are thoroughly coated.
4. Spread the mixture over the prepared baking sheet and bake 25 to 30 minutes, stirring occasionally, until all the granola is evenly browned. Remove from the oven and let the granola cool on the baking sheet for 10 minutes before stirring in the dried fruit. When completely cool, store the granola in airtight containers at room temperature for up to 1 month.

Plum-Nectarine Bread Pudding

MAKES 4 SERVINGS

Grainy, nutty breads make this a wholesome dish. However, you could also use stale low-fat muffins. It makes a satisfying weekend breakfast or brunch and is easy to make because you can assemble it the night before and bake it in the morning.

1. Preheat the oven to 350°F.
2. Spray a 9- by 13-inch baking dish with nonfat butter–flavored oil (any cooking oil spray will do in a pinch).
3. Place half of the bread pieces over the bottom of the baking dish and cover with the plum slices.
4. Combine the sugar and cinnamon and sprinkle ⅓ cup over the plums.
5. Repeat the layers by adding the remaining bread pieces, the nectarine slices, and another ⅓ cup sugar and cinnamon.
6. Whisk together the egg, the egg substitute, and the soy milk and pour over the layers. Sprinkle the top with the remaining sugar and cinnamon.
7. Bake for 55 to 60 minutes, until a toothpick inserted in the center comes out clean.
8. Remove and cool for 10 minutes (the pudding will still be warm but not red hot). Serve warm or at room temperature with vanilla yogurt.

Nonfat butter-flavored oil spray

7 large slices of oat or nut bread, cut or torn into pieces

3 large plums or plumcots, pitted and sliced

¾ cup firmly packed brown sugar

2 teaspoons ground cinnamon

3 large nectarines, pitted and sliced

1 egg

½ cup egg substitute or 2 whole eggs

1½ cups low-fat vanilla soy milk or rice milk

Vanilla yogurt, for serving

PRESERVES

There is a certain pleasure that comes with making your own frozen and canned preserves from the abundance of seasonal fruits picked up at local farmer's markets. Pulled out of the freezer or off the shelf in the dead of winter, they can be turned into a crumble, crisp, salsa, or other memorable dish that smacks of the flavors of summer.

While stone fruits are sublime in pies, tarts, crisps, and other baked desserts, a bountiful harvest can also be made into sauces, butters, chutneys, jams, and jellies. Other easy methods of preserving the harvest include canning and freezing the fruits whole, quartered, or sliced and sprinkled with sugar or bathed in sugar syrup. Tossing together a few simple ingredients such as onions, raisins, spices, peaches, and apples for a batch of homemade chutney preserves the flavors of summer and fall for the depths of winter.

There's nothing easier than making jams, chutneys, and sauces. All you do is cut up the fruits, drop them into a heavy pan with sugar and spices (plus vinegar and onions for chutneys), and cook them down slowly for about an hour. Making small batches ensures that the texture of the fruit is maintained. When large quantities are not involved, it's not even necessary to put up the fruits in canning jars and process in boiling water. Instead, they can be stored in the refrigerator for a couple of weeks or a year in the freezer.

Choose freestone fruits for ease of preparation and also when uniform slices are desired for freezing or canning. The smaller prune plums are freestone while the larger Japanese-type plums are clingstone. If you are working with clingstone fruits that don't separate easily from the pit, use them for making into sauces, butters, jams, chutneys, and other recipes where an attractive shape is not important.

Whether canning or freezing, select fruits that are firm and free of blemishes. If you can't process them the day you bring them home, keep them under refrigeration for one to two days.

Canned fruits can be stored for up to two years when not exposed to excessive heat. Fruits prepared for the freezer can be frozen for up to one year. Canning is the way to go if you don't have much space in your freezer.

Basic Canning Procedures

When preserving fruits, you will need to process the jars in a boiling-water-bath canner to ensure a long shelf life without fear of microbial contamination. If you don't have this special canner, use a large, deep pot with a tight-fitting lid and place a rack on the bottom on which to set the jars. Use standard canning jars, lids, and screw tops. Do not reuse lids from a previous canning session because the sealing material will have deteriorated slightly, greatly decreasing the chances of getting an airtight seal. You may reuse screw bands if they are not misshapen or rusted.

Fill the canner halfway with water, position the rack inside, and cover. Heat the water until it boils furiously. Meanwhile, sterilize the canning jars as follows.

Sterilizing Canning Jars

It is not necessary to sterilize jars used for food that is processed in a boiling-water bath for 10 minutes or longer. Simply wash the empty jars in soapy water and rinse thoroughly. Keep lids and rings in gently boiling water until you are ready to use them.

For boiling-water-bath processing times of less than 10 minutes, jars must be washed and sterilized. Fill the jars with hot water and submerge them in a canner filled with hot (not boiling) water, making sure the water rises 1 inch above the jar tops. At sea level, boil the jars for 10 minutes; at higher elevations, boil for an additional minute for every 1,000 feet above sea level. Use a jar lifter to remove one sterilized jar at a time; fill immediately with the prepared fruit.

Preparing Fruit

Prepare syrup, if using, and wash and prepare fruits (see Canning Quantities and Preparation Methods, page 39). Remove jars from the boiling-water bath and place on paper towels.

Stone fruits can be canned two ways (see Canning Quantities and Preparation Methods, page 39), raw pack or hot pack. With a raw pack, the fruit is placed into the jars, then the jars are covered with boiling water and processed. With a hot pack, the fruit is heated, then placed into the jars, covered with boiling water, and processed.

Filling and Processing Jars

When the water in the canner starts to boil, fill each jar with the prepared hot or cold fruit, leaving ½ to 1 inch of headspace between the fruit and the jar rim. (Headspace allows a vacuum seal to form, which is necessary to protect canned fruit from microbial contamination.) Release trapped air bubbles by sliding a plastic (nonmetallic) knife between the fruit and the side of the jar. Pour in more liquid as necessary to maintain headspace.

Wipe the rims and cover the jars with lids and screw tops. Set the jars in the canner on the rack. After adding the last jar, pour in boiling water (from a kettle) until water covers the jars by 1 inch. Cover the canner. If the water stops boiling by the time all the jars have been added, turn up the heat and wait for a full boil before timing the processing. When the water recovers a boil, reduce the heat to keep the water boiling gently.

At end of the processing time — 20 to 30 minutes for fruits in syrup (see Canning Quantities and Preparation Methods, page 39) — turn off the heat, remove the jars from the canner, and set them aside to cool. When the jars are completely cool, check the seals by pressing the center of each lid. A jar is sealed if the center is firm and slightly recessed. (See Testing for a Good Seal on page 38 for more information.)

MAKING JAMS AND JELLIES

Jams and jellies can be made from any kind of fruit as well as many vegetables — often in various and wonderful combinations. Follow the Basic Canning Procedures on page 36 as well as instructions and processing times recommended in individual recipes.

If you feel like making jams or jellies in winter — it's a lovely way to spend a cold, gloomy day indoors — pull out your frozen slices or open up a jar or can and get to it. You can use fresh, frozen, canned, or dried fruit. Once you've prepared the fruit, jam or jelly making goes very quickly. Depending on the fruits and whether or how much pectin or sugar you add, cooking times can range from 10 to 30 minutes. The basic rule for adding sugar to jams and jellies is 1 cup of liquid, diced, or crushed fruit to ¾ cup of sugar.

If you have a lot more fruit than is called for in a recipe, prepare the recipe several times rather than doubling or tripling the quantities. Crowding the pan with so much fruit and liquid will affect the texture and set of the finished product.

Testing for Jam and Jelly Set When you're not sure whether you've cooked the jam long enough to ensure a good set — you don't end up with a runny sauce! — dip a cold metal spoon into the hot mixture, raise it away from the heat, and tilt it so that the syrup runs over the side. If the syrup forms drops that merge and flow off the spoon together, the jam is ready. If the syrup flows off the spoon in a stream, it's too liquid and needs to be cooked longer.

Another method, which I prefer, is to see if it sets when dropped onto a chilled saucer. If you push your finger across the top of the jam, the surface should wrinkle. And, of course, the jam will thicken as it cools. The surest test is to use a candy thermometer to see if the jam has reached 220°F.

Jams made with juicy fruits, lower quantities of sugar, and without commercial pectin will take longer to reach setting point. If you're not adding pectin, use fruits that are firm and slightly underripe — underripe fruits contain more pectin than ripe ones. Tart plums contain more pectin than the

TESTING FOR A GOOD SEAL

After processing in a boiling-water canner, when the jars have cooled, press the center of each lid to check the seal. The jar is safely sealed if the dimple in the middle of the lid stays down. If the dimple can be bounced up and down, a tight seal has not occurred. Either reprocess in boiling water for 5 to 10 minutes (5 for ½ pints and 10 for pint jars) or store the jars in the refrigerator and use within two weeks. If the seal is good and there is no movement in the lid, label the jars with date and contents and store in a cool cupboard or pantry for up to one year.

Canning Quantities and Preparation Methods

Fruit	Quantity	Preparation	Boiling-Water Bath Raw Pack	Boiling-Water Bath Hot Pack
APRICOTS	1½–2½ pounds per quart container	Peel, if desired, by placing in wire basket and immersing in boiling water for 20 seconds, until skin starts to split. Remove and drop basket into ice-cold water. Halve and pit and quarter or slice. To retain color, drop into a solution of ascorbic acid color-keeper (refer to package directions). Remove from solution and drain.	Fill canning jars with fruit and cover with hot syrup, leaving ½ inch headspace. Process in boiling-water bath for 25 minutes (pints) or 30 minutes (quarts).	Add apricots to hot syrup and bring to a boil. Fill jars with hot fruit and syrup, leaving ½ inch headspace. Process in boiling-water bath for 20 minutes (pints) or 30 minutes (quarts).
PEACHES/ NECTARINES	2–3 pounds per quart container	Fuzzy peaches require peeling. Follow instruction for preparing apricots.	*See* Apricots.	*See* Apricots.
PLUMS	1½–2½ pounds per quart container	Clingstone plums do not separate easily. Freestone varieties are easy to halve and pit.	Fill jars with fruit and syrup, leaving ½ inch headspace. Process in boiling-water bath for 20 minutes (pints) or 25 minutes (quarts).	Cook in hot syrup in covered pan for 5 minutes over low heat. Fill jars with fruit and syrup. Leave ½ inch headspace. Process in boiling-water bath for 20 minutes (pints) or 25 minutes (quarts).

Equivalent Measures for Fruits

2–2½ pounds	3–3½ pounds	4–4½ pounds	5–5½ pounds
4 cups sliced fruit	6 cups sliced	8 cups sliced	10 cups sliced
4 cups diced	6 cups diced	8 cups diced	10 cups diced
3½ cups mashed	5 cups mashed	7 cups mashed	8½ cups mashed
3 cups puréed	4½ cups puréed	6 cups puréed	7½ cups puréed

other stone fruits. High-pectin fruits like apples (or their peels secured in cheesecloth) are often combined with low-pectin fruits and vegetables. Though you can substitute apple juice when a recipe calls for a small quantity of water, adding a few tablespoons of lemon juice instead is an excellent and sometimes necessary way to add acid to fruits low in pectin. Plums have a high pectin content, apricots a medium pectin content, and peaches and nectarines a medium-low pectin content.

Preparing Peaches Most peaches purchased in a supermarket have been washed before they are shipped. During the drying process, the fuzz is rubbed off and the skins end up being quite smooth. Buy peaches from an orchard or at a farmers' market and you'll find they have more fuzz. Wash them and dry with paper towels to remove most of the fuzz. When making jams, chutneys, and butters, there is no need to remove the skin.

Preparing Plums Most plums have flesh that clings to the stone or pit. The best way to remove the flesh is to cut the plum into wedges: Slice ½ inch wedges through the skin to the pit and remove one slice at a time. Use the same method for removing the flesh from freestone plums as recommended for freestone peaches, nectarines, and apricots: Cut along the seam of the plum to the stone and twist each half in the opposite direction. The stone can be plucked out easily.

Plum varieties differ greatly in size. Some are small enough to fit comfortably on a teaspoon, while others are as large as nectarines. Japanese plums are the largest, but even they produce a range of sizes so that 1 pound may contain as few as four plums or as many as 14. No matter the size, however, 1 pound of plums will produce about 2 cups sliced.

Making Chutney

Chutney originated in India and was very popular with British colonials. When the soldiers returned to Britain, they brought with them coveted recipes for *chatni* (the Indian word for chutney). Because some Indian ingredients were not available in the colder European climate, however, the original chatni recipes were adapted to include plums, apples, pears, peaches, apricots, bananas, and dried fruits in place of the mangoes and other tropical fruits used in India.

Chutneys are versatile preserves and can be used in many ways beyond their roles as accompaniments to simmered, grilled, and roasted foods and East Indian curries. Whether you use homemade or store bought, adding chutney to recipes and dishes is an easy way to perk up flavor.

Turn chutney into instant barbecue sauces and marinades by puréeing them with a little vinegar or fruit juice, sesame oil, and soy sauce until they reach the required consistency. If you have odds and ends of jams, throw in a spoonful to add a little sweetness. Toss with noodles, shredded chicken, scallions, and cilantro for an instant dinner or weekend lunch.

Purée chutney or stir as is into mayonnaise for a flavorful spread on grilled meat, poultry, and fish. Use it instead of butter on bread and sandwiches. Make it into a dip for vegetables or a topping for cold salmon, shrimp, or smoked trout.

Purée with olive oil to make a flavorful dressing for salad greens, shredded cabbage and carrots, warm broccoli, and grilled vegetables. Mash it with butter — ½ cup of each — and add a knob to the skillet after sautéing chicken breasts, pork medallions, or beef tenderloin to drizzle over the top of each serving. Make a sauce: After sautéing, add ½ cup of broth, wine, or apple juice and reduce by half. Stir in a couple of tablespoons of chutney butter and heat until the sauce thickens slightly.

Make enough chutney butter to keep in the refrigerator for another day. Spoon it onto wax paper and roll into a 1- to 2-inch-diameter log. Place in a airtight plastic bag and refrigerate or freeze.

Basic Freezing Procedures

To avoid freezer burn, use heavy plastic containers or special wide-topped freezer jars. Or use heavy-duty plastic freezer bags. Do not use regular glass jars. The glass may not be tempered and may crack under freezing temperatures. If using syrup, prepare ahead and cool (see page 42). If not using syrup, the fruits can be frozen dry and unsweetened, with water, or with layers of sugar.

Blanch fruits a few at a time by scalding in boiling water for 30 seconds. This not only helps to retain good color and flavor, it also makes it easier to skin apricots and peaches. (It is not necessary to remove skin from smooth nectarines, peaches, plumcots, and pluots.) To blanch, fill a large pan with water and bring to a boil. Place the fruit in a perforated metal basket and lower into the boiling water. Cover the pot and set the timer. Fill a large bowl with ice water. Remove the fruit-filled basket from the boiling water and drop the fruit into the ice water. Refresh the water for each batch of fruit.

Drain the fruit (peel peaches and apricots), cut in half, remove the pits, and quarter or slice as desired. (To prevent fruits from darkening, peel and slice only when the syrup has cooled.) Pack the fruit into the freezer containers, leaving the required headspace to allow for expansion of the fruit (see Packing Frozen Fruits, page 42). Wipe container rims and cover, pressing down to create a tight fit. If using freezer bags, press out as much air as possible before making a tight seal. Label the packs with the date and whether fruits have been packed dry or in water or syrup. Place the containers in the freezer with space between until they are frozen solid, at which time they can be moved closer together.

PACKING FROZEN FRUITS

Leaving adequate headspace will allow the fruits to expand without pushing out of plastic containers or breaking the glass of freezer jars.

Dry pack. Fruits packed without sugar or liquid require ½ inch headspace. These can be packed in plastic freezer bags, if desired. To prevent fruit from freezing together, quick-freeze in a single layer on a baking sheet, then deposit into containers. Fruits frozen with sugar or liquid will retain better texture, color, and flavor.

Water or 100 percent fruit juice. Fruits covered with water or juice require ½ inch headspace for pints and 1 inch headspace for quarts if using wide-mouthed plastic containers; ¾ inch headspace for pints and 1½ inch headspace for quarts if using narrow plastic containers or freezer jars.

Syrup pack. Fruits packed with syrup require ½ inch headspace for pints and 1 inch headspace for quarts if using widemouthed plastic containers; ¾ inch headspace for pints and 1½ inch for quarts if using narrow plastic containers or freezer jars.

Sugar pack. Fruits packed with sugar sprinkled between each layer of slices require ½ inch headspace.

MAKING SYRUP FOR CANNED OR FROZEN FRUIT

Choose a syrup that suits your taste as well as the sweet or tart flavor of the fruit. To prepare the syrup, place sugar and water in a large, heavy saucepan over medium heat. Cook until the sugar dissolves and the syrup is clear, about 10 minutes. Use hot syrup for canned fruits. Cool the syrup before adding to fruits prepared for freezing. Allow ½ to ⅔ cup of syrup for each 2 cups of fruit.

	SUGAR	WATER	YIELD
Light syrup	½–1 cup	4 cups	4½ cups
Medium syrup	2 cups	4 cups	5 cups
Heavy syrup	3–4 cups	4 cups	5½–6 cups

Apricots If desired, peel apricots. Halve, pit, and pack as recommended (see above). Use water or juice, cooled syrup, or sugar pack.

Peaches and Nectarines Peel peaches (see Canning Quantities and Preparation Methods, page 39). Halve, pit, and quarter or slice. Place halved peaches cut-side down in containers and pack as recommended (see above). Use water or juice, cooled syrup, or sugar pack.

Plums Halve and pit. Pack as recommended (see above). Use dry, cooled syrup, or sugar pack. If using a syrup pack, add ½ to 1 teaspoon of ascorbic acid per quart of syrup. If using a dry or sugar pack, sprinkle cut surfaces with lemon juice or drop fruits in a bowl of cold water and 2 tablespoons of lemon juice; drain thoroughly before sealing dry pack or layering with sugar.

Drying Fruits

Drying fruits concentrates their food values and flavors. Take plums, for example. Fresh, they are wonderfully aromatic, juicy, and flavorful, but when dried, they become veritable powerhouses of intense flavor. And while apricots, peaches, and nectarines can exude a heady fragrance when they are fresh and perfectly ripe, their flesh also develops a deeper flavor when dried.

For this reason, and the fact that dried fruits are a good source of fiber, iron, potassium, and increased values of vitamin A and B vitamins (drying decreases their content of vitamin C), they are perfect choices for adding extra flavor and color to savory as well as sweet dishes. For example, toss them into a pan of sliced onions, carrots, and beets, drizzle with olive oil, and roast at 350°F for 45 minutes. Roughly chop dried peaches, apricots, or plums and stir into stuffing, rice, couscous, and salad dishes. Or dice and fold into cake, muffin, and bread batters.

You might want to try your hand at drying your own fruit once you know how easy it is. If you get hooked and decide to dry large quantities, you may end up buying a commercial dehydrator.

For small quantities, however, your oven will work just as well.

OVEN DRYING

Choose firm, unblemished plums, apricots, peaches, or nectarines. Cut them into thin slices and spread in single layers on baking trays or screen mesh. Place trays or screens in the oven on separate shelves and leave the door ajar to allow for air circulation. Turn the oven to its lowest setting, or no higher than 140 degrees, and allow the slices to dry until they are leathery but pliable and still slightly sticky when cut into — there should be no moisture on the outside. Turn the slices occasionally so they dry evenly. Variations in ovens and moisture of fruits will affect the length of the drying process, which may take from 4 to 24 hours. Using screen mesh instead of solid trays allows for better air circulation and speeds up the drying process.

Apricot-Prune Chutney

MAKES 3 CUPS

12 ounces dried apricots, chopped (about 2¼ cups)

1 large onion, chopped (about 1 cup)

4 ounces pitted prunes, cut up (about ¾ cup)

½ cup firmly packed brown sugar

½ cup apple juice

½ cup cider vinegar

1 tablespoon grated fresh ginger

Zest of about ⅓ orange (1 tablespoon)

1 teaspoon ground allspice

1. Combine all the ingredients in a 4-quart heavy saucepan. Bring to a boil over high heat.
2. Reduce the heat to low, cover, and simmer for 1 hour, stirring occasionally.
3. Remove from the heat, cool, and spoon into airtight jars or containers and refrigerate. Because it is made from dried fruit, this chutney will keep for months in the refrigerator.

Simply Bishop's Pickled Peaches

MAKES 4 SERVINGS

These pickles make a great side dish for roast duck, turkey, and pork.

6 large peaches, peeled and pitted

1 cup apple cider vinegar

1 cup water

½ cup sugar

1 cinnamon stick

6 whole allspice berries

Pinch of ground cloves, no more than ⅛ teaspoon

1. Cut the peaches into ½-inch slices and place in a bowl.
2. Bring the vinegar, water, sugar, cinnamon, allspice, and cloves to a boil in a saucepan over medium-high heat.
3. Pour the mixture over the peaches. Allow the peaches to cool in the pickling syrup before refrigerating. Refrigerate for up to 1 week.

Slow-Cooker Preserves

8 cups sliced peaches,
nectarines, plums, plumcots,
or a combination

3–4 cups sugar
(tart plums will demand the
extra ½–1 cup)

½ tablespoon ground
cinnamon

½ teaspoon ground ginger

2 tablespoons apple juice,
freshly squeezed lemon juice
(about ⅔ lemon), or water

When there are so many demands on your time and yet you have a few pounds of fruit that needs to be used before it spoils, slow cooking can provide an easy solution. Depending on how juicy the fruits are, you might prefer to turn this into a sauce.

1. Drop the sliced fruit into the ceramic container of a slow cooker.
2. Mix the sugar, cinnamon, and ginger in a small bowl. Toss with the fruit. Drizzle the apple juice over the top.
3. Cook, covered, on low heat for 10 hours, or until the jam passes one of the doneness tests on page 38. Alternatively, cook over low heat for 3 hours, then increase the heat to high and cook 4 hours longer, or until the fruit passes one of the same doneness tests.
4. When cool, remove the fruit (use a slotted spoon if there is a lot of juice, and reserve the juice) and purée in a blender or food processor. Add the reserved juice as desired. Alternatively, smash the fruit with a fork to create the consistency of a chunkier preserve.
5. Spoon the jam into airtight containers and store in the refrigerator for 1 to 2 weeks or in the freezer for up to 1 year. Leave at least ½ inch of headspace when storing in the freezer.

Microwave Apricot Jam

Because microwaves vary in size and wattage, make this small-batch recipe first before attempting to double it. Besides, it's so easy, it takes no time at all to make small batches as needed.

Use ripe, canned, or frozen apricots. If you prefer, substitute fresh, frozen, or canned peaches. Thaw if frozen; drain if canned. Be sure to reserve the juice.

1 pound apricots, pitted and sliced (about 2 cups)

¾ cup sugar

Juice of about ⅓ lemon (1 tablespoon)

1. Crush the apricots with a potato masher and place in a 2-quart microwave-safe dish. Stir in the sugar and lemon juice.
2. Microwave, uncovered, on HIGH (100 percent power) for 3 to 4 minutes. Remove and stir the mixture thoroughly. Microwave for 4 minutes longer. Remove and stir again. The mixture should have thickened.
3. Allow to cool. If the jam seems a little too thick, add a splash of the reserved juice or apple juice or lemon juice and stir to make a softer consistency.
4. Spoon into an airtight container or a glass jar and store in the refrigerator for up to 2 weeks.

Refrigerator Winter Peach–Apricot Sauce

2 cans (15 ounces each) sliced peaches, drained (reserve or discard juice as desired)

1 can (8 ounces) apricot nectar

8 ounces dried apricots, chopped (about 1½ cups)

2 tablespoons chopped crystallized ginger

⅓ cup sugar

2 tablespoons whiskey or brandy

Serve this as a savory or sweet sauce. Cook it down a little longer for a thicker consistency. This quantity will allow you to freeze 2 cups for future use.

1. Coarsely chop the peach slices and place in a large (about 4-quart) heavy saucepan over medium high heat.
2. Add the apricot nectar, dried apricots, and crystallized ginger. Stir the mixture until thoroughly combined. Cover and bring to a boil.
3. Reduce the heat to medium-low and allow the mixture to bubble gently for 5 minutes. Crush it with a fork and stir in the sugar and whiskey.
4. Increase the heat to high and return the mixture to a boil. Reduce the heat to medium-low and cook, uncovered, about 20 minutes, stirring frequently, until the mixture thickens.
5. Remove from the heat and cool before spooning into airtight containers or jars for storage in the refrigerator or freezer. Leave at least ½ inch of headspace in the freezer containers. Refrigerate up to 1 month or freeze up to 1 year.

Plum Jam

Tart plums are best when cooked. Greengages and damsons are especially wonderful when made into jam, and because they are naturally acidic, they contain a lot of pectin. I like my jam chunky, but if you prefer a smoother jam, purée in a processor when the plums have cooked to the soft stage.

2 pounds tart plums, pitted and cut in quarters

3–4 tablespoons water

2 pounds sugar

1. Place the plums in a large, heavy pan and add enough water to cover the bottom of the pan. Bring to a boil over medium heat, reduce the heat to low, cover, and simmer 15 minutes, or until the plums are soft. (If desired, purée in a food processor.)

2. Increase the heat to high and return to a boil. Stir in the sugar. Return to a hard boil and cook, stirring, for 4 minutes, until the sugar is dissolved.

3. Remove the pan from the heat and skim off the foam with a large metal spoon. Ladle the jam into hot, sterilized half-pint jars, leaving a ½-inch headspace. (Using a widemouthed-funnel makes it an easier and cleaner job when filling the smaller, half-pint canning jars.) Run a rubber spatula around the inside of the jars to release air bubbles. Wipe rims with a clean cloth and cap according to the manufacturer's instructions. Process 5 minutes in a boiling-water-bath canner (see page 37). Store the jars in a cool cupboard.

Nectarine-Blueberry Jam

3 pounds nectarines, pitted, sliced, and coarsely chopped (about 5 cups)

2 cups blueberries

1 package (1.75 ounces) powdered fruit pectin

Juice of about 1 lemon (3 tablespoons)

1 cinnamon stick

5 cups sugar

Use peaches if they are more plentiful.

1. Bring to a boil the nectarines, blueberries, pectin, lemon juice, and cinnamon in a large, heavy kettle over medium-high heat. Crush some of the fruit with a potato masher once the mixture is hot. Allow the mixture to come to a rolling boil for 1 minute, stirring constantly.
2. Stir in the sugar and return to a rolling boil for 4 minutes, stirring constantly, until the sugar is dissolved.
3. Remove from the heat and discard the cinnamon stick. Skim off the foam, if necessary.
4. Ladle the jam into hot, sterilized pint jars (you will need seven or eight jars) with the aid of a widemouthed-funnel, leaving a ½-inch headspace. Run a rubber spatula around the inside of the jars to release air bubbles. Wipe the rim of the each jar with a clean cloth and cap according to the manufacturer's instructions. Seal with lids and screw bands.
5. Process 10 minutes in a boiling-water-bath canner (see page 37).
6. Remove the jars and cool the jam. Check that the lids have perfect seals (see page 38). Store the jars in a cool cupboard.

Peach-Orange Marmalade

Substitute nectarines if desired. For variation, use two oranges and two large lemons — the slightly tarter flavor goes well with sweet potatoes and savory biscuits. It also can be added to marinades and glazes for roasting Cornish hens, duck, turkey, or chicken.

Juice of 4 medium oranges (1⅓ to 2 cups)

Zest of 4 medium oranges (¼ to ½ cup)

3 pounds peaches, pitted and coarsely diced

6 cups sugar

1. Bring all of the ingredients to a full boil in a large, heavy pan over high heat. Continue to boil, uncovered, stirring frequently, about 20 minutes, until a candy thermometer registers 220°F or the marmalade sets when dropped onto a chilled saucer.

3. Remove the pan from the heat and skim off the foam with a large metal spoon. Ladle into hot, sterilized half-pint jars, leaving a ½-inch headspace. (Using a widemouthed-funnel makes it an easier and cleaner job when filling the smaller, half-pint canning jars.) Run a rubber spatula around the inside of the jars to release air bubbles. Wipe the rims of the jars with a clean cloth and cap each jar according to the manufacturer's instructions.

4. Process 5 minutes in a boiling-water-bath canner (see page 37). Store in a cool cupboard.

Peach Butter

4–5 pounds peaches (8–10 large peaches), pitted and chopped (or substitute 8 to 9 cups frozen slices, thawed)

¼ cup peach nectar or apple juice

1 pound sugar (2½ cups)

1 teaspoon ground cinnamon

Make this with nectarines, apricots, plums, or plumcots — or half peach and half plum. Depending on how sweet and how much juice runs out of the fruit, add an extra ¼ cup of juice for firm, less juicy fruits and ½ cup sugar or honey for less sweet fruits.

1. Place the peaches and nectar in a large, heavy pan over medium-high heat. When the peaches start to bubble around the edges, reduce the heat and cover the pan. Simmer for 15 minutes, stirring halfway through.

2. Spoon into a blender and purée until smooth. Pour the purée back into the pan and stir in the sugar and cinnamon.

3. Simmer, uncovered, over low heat, stirring occasionally, until the mixture is thick, about 1½ hours. Alternatively, pour the mixture into a roasting pan and bake, uncovered, at 350°F for about 1½ hours, stirring occasionally.

4. To can the butter, remove from the heat and ladle into hot, sterilized pint jars, leaving ½ inch headspace. Run a rubber spatula around the inside of the jar to release air bubbles. Wipe the rims with a clean cloth and cap each jar according to the manufacturer's instructions.

5. Process 10 minutes in a boiling-water-bath canner (see page 37).

6. If preferred, freeze the butter for up to 1 year (see basic freezing procedures on page 41).

Fruit Leather

*Make this with peaches, nectarines, apricots, or plumcots —
whichever fruit your family loves and is in season. This makes
a sweet snack and adds a lovely chewiness to salads and grain
dishes. Simply dice and sprinkle over or stir into the dish.*

1. Preheat the oven to 150°F.
2. Purée the sliced fruit in a food processor or blender.
3. Place the puréed fruit in a large, heavy pan. Add the sugar and
   bring to a boil over medium heat. Stir until the sugar has dissolved,
   about 3 minutes. Remove from the heat and allow to cool until just
   barely warm.
4. Line three jelly-roll pans with wax paper and spread with the fruit
   mixture so that it is ⅛ to ¼ inch thick and comes to within ½ inch
   of the edges.
5. Bake with the door propped slightly open (to allow the moisture to
   escape) for about 3 hours. The fruit leather should be slightly
   sticky and pull away from the wax paper. (If not, leave it in the
   oven until it does start to pull away.)
6. Lift up about 1 inch and start rolling it over in the wax paper. Place
   in a plastic bag or wrap in plastic. Store in the refrigerator for up to
   1 month or in the freezer for up to 6 months.

4 pounds fully ripe fruit,
pitted and sliced (about
8 cups)

1 cup sugar

1 teaspoon ground cinnamon

Barbecue Sauce

MAKES ABOUT 3½ CUPS

Use juicy ripe fruit for this no-cook sauce.

1 pound plumcots, plums, peaches, apricots, or other stone fruit, pitted and cut in quarters

2 cups applesauce

½ cup honey teriyaki sauce

1 clove elephant garlic

1 teaspoon ground or grated ginger

½ teaspoon ground cinnamon

¼ teaspoon cayenne pepper

¼ teaspoon ground cloves

1. Place all the ingredients in a food processor or blender and purée until smooth.
2. Adjust the thickness, if you wish, by adding extra fruit or a few tablespoons of teriyaki sauce or peach nectar. Add more spices to your liking.
3. Refrigerate in an airtight container and use within 1 week.

Any-Fruit Ketchup

MAKES 2 PINTS

2 pounds stone fruit, pitted and sliced

2 cloves garlic

1½ cups brown sugar

1 cup cider vinegar

1 teaspoon ground allspice

½ teaspoon ground cinnamon

½ teaspoon ground ginger

¼ teaspoon cayenne pepper

1. Purée the fruit and garlic until smooth.
2. Pour into a heavy pan; stir in the sugar, vinegar, allspice, cinnamon, ginger, and cayenne.
3. Bring to a boil over high heat. Reduce the heat to medium and cook 20 to 30 minutes, stirring occasionally, until the mixture is thick.
4. Using a widemouthed funnel, ladle the mixture into hot, sterilized jars. Run a spatula around the inside to release air bubbles. Wipe the rims and cap each jar according to the manufacturer's instructions.
5. Process half-pints for 5 minutes and pints for 10 minutes in a boiling-water-bath canner (see page 37).

Plum-Apple Chutney

Depending on the season, substitute apricots or nectarines for the plums. You might also want to turn this recipe into barbecue sauce by cooking it down for less time, stopping before it becomes thick, or adding a little hot apple or orange juice to thin it. Simply purée the hot chutney in batches in a blender and pour into the hot, sterilized jars.

1. Combine all the ingredients in a large, heavy pan, cover, and bring to a boil over high heat.
2. Remove the cover, reduce the heat to low, and simmer for about 2 hours, or until the chutney is thick and tender.
3. Ladle into hot, sterilized pint jars, leaving a ½ inch headspace. Run a rubber spatula around the inside of the jars to release air bubbles. Wipe the rims of the jars with a clean cloth and cap each jar according to the manufacturer's instructions.
4. Process 10 minutes in a boiling-water-bath canner (see page 37). Store in a cool cupboard.

3 pounds plums, pitted and chopped (about 6 cups)

6 large apples (Fuji, Jonagold, and Winesap work well), peeled, cored, and diced

2 cups apple cider vinegar

8 ounces dried apricots, chopped (about 1½ cups)

1 medium red onion, chopped

1–1½ pounds sugar (use the greater quantity if the plums are really tart)

1½ teaspoons ground cinnamon

½ teaspoon ground cloves

SALADS, SANDWICHES, AND SOUPS

Apricots, plums, peaches, and nectarines lend themselves to all kinds of dishes. Their colors, textures, and shapes make them natural choices for adding to salads and soups. They can also be the unexpected and delicious flavor in tortilla wraps, quesadillas, and sandwiches.

Chicken Salad with Nectarine and Kiwi

MAKES 4-6 SERVINGS

This salad is as pretty as it is tasty. Make it a summer dinner for four or for a crowd — the chicken breasts cook in little time and the rest goes together easily. If you are cooking for a crowd, prepare the chicken breasts and the salad dressing a day ahead.

1. Place the nectar, vinegar, 3 tablespoons of the sesame oil, and the soy sauce, pickled ginger, garlic, and wasabi paste in a screw-top jar. Shake vigorously to mix.

2. Place the remaining 2 tablespoons of sesame oil and the ground ginger in a shallow dish. Add the chicken and turn to coat each side with the oil.

3. Spray a large heavy skillet with cooking oil spray and place over high heat. When hot, add the coated chicken breasts and elephant garlic. Cook the chicken 5 to 6 minutes on each side, until no longer pink inside. Remove the chicken and garlic to a plate.

4. When cool, cut the chicken breasts into 1-inch pieces and place in a bowl with the nectarines, pepper, and scallions. Pour ¼ cup of the nectar dressing over the chicken mixture and toss to coat.

5. Place the spinach on a serving plate and toss with 2 tablespoons of dressing. Top with the chicken mixture and spoon the kiwi into the middle. Pass the remaining salad dressing at the table.

¼ cup peach or apricot nectar

3 tablespoons seasoned rice wine vinegar

5 tablespoons roasted light sesame oil

2 tablespoons reduced-sodium soy sauce

1 tablespoon chopped pickled ginger

2 cloves garlic

2 teaspoons wasabi paste

½ teaspoon ground ginger

4 boneless, skinless chicken breasts

Cooking oil spray

1 large clove elephant garlic, thinly sliced lengthwise

2 nectarines, pitted and diced

1 large red bell pepper, diced

3 scallions, sliced

4 cups baby spinach leaves or mixed spring greens

2 kiwis, peeled and diced

Plum, Carrot, and Hearts of Palm Salad

MAKES 8 SERVINGS

½ cup canola oil

¼ cup seasoned rice vinegar

2 tablespoons toasted sesame seeds (see Toasting Seeds and Nuts, page 88)

½-inch piece of fresh gingerroot, washed and sliced (peeled if desired)

2 tablespoons chopped umeboshi or neri-ume plums (Asian pickled plums in a jar)

1 tablespoon sweet mirin (available in Asian food shops)

¼ teaspoon freshly ground black pepper

¼ teaspoon salt (or to taste)

6 cups mixed Asian spring greens (8 ounces)

4 large, firm ripe plums or pluots, pitted and thinly sliced

1½ cups sliced hearts of palm

½ sweet onion, cut in two lengthwise and thinly sliced

2 large carrots, peeled and shredded

This brightly colored salad not only dresses up the table, but is also high in antioxidants. There will be salad dressing left over for use on other mixed greens or vegetables.

1. Process the oil, vinegar, toasted sesame seeds, gingerroot, umeboshi, mirin, pepper, and salt in a blender until smooth.
2. Place the spring greens in a large salad bowl and toss with 2 to 3 tablespoons of the dressing.
3. In another bowl, toss the plums, hearts of palm, and onion with 2 tablespoons of the dressing and layer over the spring greens.
4. Toss the grated carrots with 2 tablespoons of the dressing and spoon around the edges of the salad bowl.

PEELING JUICY FRUITS

If you've ever peeled tomatoes, you already know how to peel peaches, nectarines, plums, and apricots. Prepare a bowl of ice-cold water. Bring a pot of water to a boil and immerse the fruit for 20 to 30 seconds. Remove with tongs and drop into the ice-cold water. Pick up the fruit and lift off the skin with a small paring knife, starting at the stem end. The advantage of blanching peaches and nectarines is that the slices won't turn dark as readily, which is particularly desirable when using them in salads, on ice cream, or for garnish. To keep them even brighter, sprinkle with a little lime or lemon juice, or drop the slices into a bowl of cold water containing 1 tablespoon of lemon juice.

Tofu and Plum Noodle Salad

If desired, substitute the sweet plums with sliced ripe apricots.

1. Purée the garlic, cilantro, sesame oil, sesame paste, soy sauce, miso, rice vinegar, and hot sesame oil in a blender until smooth. Add the green tea and blend again until smooth. You may add a tablespoon or more of water to make a thinner paste or adjust the flavor if you wish.

2. Drain and press the tofu between several changes of paper towels to remove excess moisture. Cut into 1-inch cubes.

3. Spray a skillet with garlic-flavored cooking oil spray and place over medium heat. When hot, add the tofu and stir-fry for 2 to 3 minutes, until lightly golden. Remove from the heat and toss with 2 tablespoons of the dressing.

4. Cook the spaghetti according to package directions, drain, and rinse with cold water. Return to the saucepan and toss with ¼ cup of the dressing.

5. Place the bean sprouts, scallions, and cucumber in a large shallow serving bowl and toss with 2 tablespoons of the dressing. Layer the noodles and tofu over the top and sprinkle with the plums. Pour the remaining dressing over the top.

3 cloves garlic

Small handful cilantro leaves

¼ cup roasted dark sesame oil

¼ cup sesame paste or peanut butter

¼ cup reduced-sodium soy sauce

2 tablespoons white miso paste

2 tablespoons seasoned rice vinegar or cider vinegar

½–1 teaspoon hot sesame oil or 1 teaspoon chili paste (or to taste)

½ cup green tea

16 ounces extra-firm tofu

Garlic-flavored cooking oil spray

8 ounces thin spaghetti

2 cups fresh bean sprouts

6 scallions, sliced

½ small cucumber, peeled and julienned

1 cup Italian or cherry plums, pitted and quartered

Brown Rice, Apricot, and Seitan Salad

3 cups cooked brown rice, cooled to room temperature

¾ cup chopped dried apricots

1 Asian pear, cored and chopped

½ small red onion, chopped

1½ cups nonfat plain or peach yogurt

3 tablespoons peach or apricot jam

1 tablespoon dried oregano

1 teaspoon ground cumin

1 teaspoon curry

½ teaspoon salt

½ teaspoon freshly ground black pepper

½ cup pine nuts

1 teaspoon olive oil

2 packages (8 ounces each) of seitan, teriyaki or chicken flavor

6 cups arugula leaves or spring greens (about 8 ounces)

This is the kind of dish that lends itself to various foolproof makeovers. Toss in a cup or two of left over chicken, turkey, or pork and use dried plums or peaches in place of the dried apricots. If it's around Thanksgiving, add a cup of dried or chopped fresh cranberries.

1. Place the cooked rice, ½ cup of the apricots, the pear, and onion into a large bowl and combine.

2. Whisk together the yogurt, jam, oregano, cumin, curry, salt, and pepper in a small bowl. Spoon half of the yogurt mixture over the rice and stir until thoroughly combined.

3. Toast the pine nuts (see Toasting Seeds and Nuts, page 88). Remove to a small plate.

4. Pour 1 teaspoon of the olive oil into the hot skillet. Add the seitan and cook 2 minutes on each side. Reduce the heat to low, cover, and allow to heat through for 5 minutes. Remove from the skillet and cut into thin slices.

5. Line a serving plate with the arugula, spoon the rice mixture into the middle, layer the seitan on top, and sprinkle the pine nuts over everything. Spoon the rest of the yogurt sauce around the edge of the plate, over the greens.

Nectarine-Plum-Broccoli Slaw

MAKES 12–16 SERVINGS

Next time you can't resist buying hard nectarines, peaches, or plums from the supermarket, don't wait for them to turn into mealy specimens lacking in sweetness. Instead, buy them with the idea of cooking them for a side dish or using them in salads like this slaw. Shred the carrots and fennel bulb with a mandoline or sharp knife or in a food processor fitted with a shredder disk.

1. Place the plums, nectarines, carrots, fennel, and broccoli slaw in a large salad bowl.
2. Purée the oil, basil, orange juice, pecans, mustard, zest, pepper, and salt in a blender until smooth.
3. Pour half the dressing over the slaw mixture and toss together. Refrigerate the remaining dressing in a pitcher or glass jar. Cover the bowl of slaw with plastic wrap and refrigerate for 2 hours for the flavors to blend.
4. Remove the slaw and dressing from the refrigerator 30 minutes before serving. Shake the dressing vigorously and pour over the slaw or pass around the table.

1 pound very firm red or purple plums, sliced from the pit and julienned

1 pound very firm nectarines, halved, pitted, and julienned

2 medium-sized carrots, peeled and shredded

1 fennel bulb, shredded (first remove outer layers and hard core)

2 cups packaged shredded broccoli slaw (available with other vegetables in your supermarket's cold case)

½ cup olive oil

½ cup sweet basil leaves

Juice of about 1 medium orange (½ cup)

¼ cup pecan halves

2 tablespoons honey mustard

Zest of about ⅔ medium orange (2 teaspoons)

¼ teaspoon freshly ground black pepper (or to taste)

¼ teaspoon salt

Chutney Salad Dressing

MAKES 1½ CUPS

½ cup **Apricot Relish** (see page 75) or **McCrady's Peach-Thyme Chutney** (see page 103)

½ cup **apricot or peach nectar or carrot juice**

2–3 cloves **garlic**

¼ cup **balsamic or seasoned rice vinegar or 2 tablespoons each**

½ cup **olive oil**

1. Place all ingredients in a screw-top jar and shake vigorously to mix. Alternatively, purée in a blender to make a smooth dressing.
2. Refrigerate for up to 1 month.

Lime-Peach Vinaigrette

MAKES 1½ CUPS

Juice of about 2 limes (½ cup)

1 cup **sliced peaches** (fresh, frozen [thawed], or canned in light syrup [drained])

½ cup **olive oil**

Juice of about ¼ lemon (2 teaspoons)

1 tablespoon **honey**

1 tablespoon **Dijon mustard**

2 cloves **garlic**

1. Process all the ingredients in a blender until smooth.
2. Refrigerate for up to 1 month

JOHN BISHOP

Executive Chef: BISHOP'S RESTAURANT, Vancouver, British Columbia

John Bishop has cooked around the world with many famous chefs, including Julia Child and Roger Verge, names he respected when he was just a young lad growing up in Newtown, in the beautiful valleys of Montgomeryshire, Mid Wales. Bishop became enamored of cooking as a child, helping his mother in the kitchen and his father in the vegetable garden. "I knew early on that I wanted to cook and when I was 16, I signed up at the new hotel school in Llandudno, on the north coast," he says. After hotel school, he worked at several restaurants in Britain before moving to Vancouver in 1973. After 10 years as head chef at Umberto's, Bishop left to open his own place.

Today, as owner and executive chef of the small but elegant Bishop's, John Bishop is a culinary leader credited for the contributions he has made to the Pacific Northwest style of cooking. He was recognized by *Food & Wine* in its 2003 annual "Best of the Best" for his cookbook, *Simply Bishop's* (coauthored with his head chef, Dennis Green), and for his focus on fresh Pacific Northwest ingredients.

Located in the Kitsilano area of Vancouver, Bishop's is one of the most highly regarded restaurants in the region. Since its opening in 1985, Bishop's has won many awards plus top ratings in all respected North American restaurant guides. Bishop's reputation has attracted heads of state, celebrities, and food lovers from near and far.

Apart from the restaurant's warm, tasteful decor, exceptional service, and, of course, the innovative and eclectic cuisine, the restaurant also has a vast wine list. "I began learning about wine in the early 1960s in Ireland. I had this wonderful experience running the Man Friday restaurant in Kinsale, creating a menu of the local fish and game and a wine list that was amazingly wide ranging," said Bishop.

John Bishop's philosophy of cooking — use the freshest seasonal ingredients and keep preparations simple — became even more important to him after his role in the 2002 Canadian documentary *Deconstructing Supper,* a culinary journey around the world to learn what people are growing and cooking. Working on the film made Bishop more aware of where his food comes from.

Bishop's imaginative seasonal menu specializes in Pacific Northwest cuisine with Asian influences — for example, crab choder with lemongrass and coconut, pesto-crusted halibut with red lentil dahl, and dishes containing plums, peaches, and apricots. John and Dennis share some of their peachy recipes in this book: Plum Soup with Tarragon and Mascarpone (page 64), Split Roast Chicken with Roasted Potatoes and Pickled Peaches (page 113) or Roast Pork Tenderloin with Apricot and Sage Stuffing (page 114), Bishop's Chèvre Cheesecake with Apricot Brandy Syrup (page 150).

Bishop's Chilled Peach and Honey Soup

MAKES 4 SERVINGS

4 large peaches, peeled, halved, and pitted

1 cup fruity white wine

½ cup honey

1 teaspoon grated fresh ginger

1 cinnamon stick

3–4 leaves fresh lemon verbena

2 cups sparkling mineral water

½ cup plain yogurt for garnish

¼ cup chopped fresh mint for garnish

Like other fresh produce used at Bishop's Restaurant in Vancouver, the peaches are from British Columbia. The Okanagan Valley peaches in this recipe are tree ripened, just the way proprietor John Bishop and chef Dennis Green prefer them. This is from their book Simply Bishop's. *They use lemon verbena in this recipe — a leafy herb that is easy to grow and reseeds prolifically. If you don't grow it and can't find it, substitute a few strands of fresh lemon zest.*

1. Bring the peaches, wine, honey, ginger, cinnamon stick, and lemon verbena to a boil in a soup pot and cook over medium-high heat for 30 minutes. Discard the lemon verbena leaves and cinnamon.
2. Remove from the heat and cool for 15 minutes.
3. Purée in a blender or food processor until smooth. Transfer to a covered container and chill in the refrigerator.
4. Before serving, add the sparkling mineral water to the peach purée and whisk together. Ladle soup into chilled bowls and garnish with a dollop of plain yogurt and a sprinkling of mint.

Bishop's Plum Soup with Tarragon and Mascarpone

MAKES 4 SERVINGS

Dawne Gourley, former soup maker at Bishop's Restaurant in Vancouver, dreamed up this recipe. Proprietor John Bishop also makes it with blueberries and cherries, whichever are in season.

1. Bring the plums, water, wine, sugar, lemon juice, lemon zest, tarragon, and thyme to a boil in a large saucepan over medium-high heat.
2. Reduce the heat to low and simmer, uncovered, until the fruit is soft, about 5 minutes. Remove from the heat and cool for 15 minutes.
3. Transfer the fruit mixture to a blender or food processor and add the mascarpone. Purée until smooth.
4. Refrigerate until completely chilled.
5. To serve, ladle the soup into bowls and garnish with a swirl of the yogurt in the center.

1 pound plums, pits removed and cut into chunks (2 cups)

1 cup water

1 cup dry white wine

½ cup sugar or honey

Juice of 2 lemons (about 6 tablespoons)

Zest of 2 lemons (about 2 tablespoons)

1 tablespoon fresh tarragon leaves

1 teaspoon fresh thyme leaves

1 cup mascarpone

¼ cup plain yogurt for garnish

Beet Soup with Nectarines

MAKES 4 SERVINGS

2 pounds fresh beets or
2 (15-ounce) cans beets,
drained

¼ cup water

2 cups peach nectar

2 tablespoons balsamic or
apple cider vinegar

½ cup light sour cream

2 white or yellow nectarines,
pitted and diced

1 tablespoon snipped fresh
chives or dill

This soup is delicious served cold. However, you can also heat the soup before topping with sour cream and diced peaches. When cooking fresh beets, don't cut off the root ends or stems too close or they will bleed.

1. Wash and trim beets leaving about ¼ inch of tops and the straggly root portion. Place in a 2-quart microwavable dish with the water. Cover with plastic wrap and microwave on HIGH 15 to 18 minutes. Allow to stand, covered, for 5 minutes. When cool enough to handle, simply slip off the skins and slice the beets.

2. Place the beets in a blender or food processor with the peach nectar and vinegar and purée. Chill for at least 1 hour.

TO SERVE: Pour the beet soup into four bowls. Spoon 1 tablespoon of sour cream over the top of each and swirl lightly into the soup. Spoon 1 tablespoon of sour cream into the center of each bowl and surround with 3 or 4 spoons of diced nectarine. Sprinkle with chives and serve immediately.

Apricot and Mushroom Brie Quesadillas

MAKES 4–8 SERVINGS

While these quesadillas make great snacks and appetizers, I also serve them when people drop in unexpectedly for lunch. And even though they're so easy to make, they never fail to impress.

1. Spread each tortilla with 2 tablespoons of the chutney. Place two or three slices of cheese on half of each tortilla (leave one side empty for folding over the filling) and top with the apricot slices divided evenly among them. Fold over each tortilla to form a semicircle, enclosing the filling. Press the sides together gently.

2. Lightly spray a large skillet with cooking oil spray and turn the heat to medium. Place two prepared tortillas in the skillet with the cheese side down. Cook 2 minutes; carefully turn the quesadillas and cook the other side for 2 minutes, until the tortillas are lightly browned and the cheese melted.

3. Remove to a serving plate and repeat with the remaining two tortillas. (If necessary, to avoid crowding the skillet and making it difficult to turn the quesadillas, cook them one at a time.) Slice the warm quesadillas into two or four wedges.

4 flour tortillas, 8 inches each

½ cup fresh chutney (I recommend McCrady's Peach-Thyme Chutney, page 103)

4 ounces mushroom Brie or Saga blue, cut in 8–12 thin slices

4 ripe apricots, pitted and cut in ¼-inch slices

Cooking oil spray

Roasted Plum and Goat Cheese Quesadillas

MAKES 4–8 SERVINGS

Cooking oil spray

1 medium-sized sweet onion, cut in half and thinly sliced

2 teaspoons olive or canola oil

½–1 teaspoon chili powder

1 log of goat cheese (4–6 ounces) cut into four lengthwise slices, each slice cut in two

4 flour tortillas, 8 inches each

¼ cup shredded cilantro leaves

8 medium-sized plums, cut in half, roasted firm (see page 109) and thinly sliced

1 cup salsa (optional; try Kate Zurschmeide's Peach Tomato Salsa page 76, or Apricot-Avocado Salsa page 80.)

If roasting the plums doesn't fit your schedule, cut each into six to eight slices and soften them in the skillet with the onions.

1. Preheat the oven to 425°F. Lightly spray a baking sheet with cooking oil spray.
2. Heat the oil in a large skillet over medium-high heat. Add the onion, sprinkle with the chili powder, and stir-fry for 5 minutes, until the slices are soft and golden on the edges.
3. Place two pieces of cheese on half of each tortilla (leave one side empty for folding over the filling) and sprinkle with the cilantro. Top the cheese with the onion and the roasted plums. Fold over the tortilla to form a semicircle, enclosing the plum mixture. Press the sides together gently.
4. Place the tortillas on the baking sheet. Spray the tops with cooking oil spray and bake for 5 minutes.
5. Remove from the oven and, when cool enough to handle, cut each quesadilla in half. Serve warm with the salsa on the side (if using).

Chicken-Feta-Plum Pita

MAKES 4 SERVINGS

⅓ cup low-fat mayonnaise

1 tablespoon snipped chives or scallion greens

1 teaspoon wasabi paste (green horseradish) or 1 tablespoon Dijon mustard

1 cup shredded lettuce leaves

2 medium-sized, firm sweet plums, pitted and sliced

¼ cup crumbled feta or blue cheese

2 boned chicken breasts, fully cooked and cut in thin slices

¼ teaspoon salt

4 pita pockets (6 inches each)

1. Mix the mayonnaise, chives, and wasabi in a medium-sized bowl. Stir in the lettuce, plums, and cheese until evenly coated with mayonnaise.
2. Season the chicken with the salt and place three slices in each pita round. Spoon one quarter of the salad mixture on top of each.
3. If desired, microwave each filled pita for 30 seconds on HIGH.

Ham and Apricot Relish Sandwiches

MAKES 4 SERVINGS

If you wish, add a layer of Muenster cheese to each sandwich.

¼ cup reduced-fat mayonnaise

8 large slices nutty whole wheat or oat bread

½ small cucumber, peeled and cut in thin slices

4 Boston lettuce leaves

4–6 ounces honey-roasted ham slices

½ cup Apricot Relish (page 75)

1. Spread the mayonnaise over the eight slices of bread.
2. Layer four bread slices with the cucumber, lettuce, and ham evenly divided among each.
3. Spread 2 tablespoons of the relish over the top of the ham slices and top with the remaining bread slices.
4. Press the sandwiches together and cut in half diagonally.

Grilled Cheese-Chutney Sandwich

MAKES 2-4 SERVINGS

¾ **cup mix of shredded Mexican Cheddar and Monterey Jack**

1 tablespoon low-fat mayonnaise

½ **teaspoon freshly ground black pepper (or to taste)**

4 large slices nutty oatmeal or whole-grain bread

¼ **cup Plum-Apple Chutney (page 54) or other chutney**

Olive oil cooking spray

This is a flavorful variation on the basic grilled cheese sandwich. Serve it for lunch or as a snack or appetizer. If you wish, add a slice of ham to each sandwich.

1. Mix the cheese, mayonnaise, and pepper in a medium-sized bowl.
2. Spread each slice of the bread with 1 tablespoon of the chutney. Spoon the cheese mixture on two slices of the bread, spreading it out evenly. Top with the remaining two slices of bread and press together.
3. Spray a griddle or large skillet with olive oil or butter-flavored cooking oil spray and turn to medium-high heat. When the oil starts to sizzle, about 1 minute, cook the sandwiches until browned, about 3 minutes.
4. Move the sandwiches quickly to a plate, spray the uncooked top side of the sandwiches with the cooking oil, return to the pan, and cook on the other side 2 to 3 minutes longer, or until the bread is golden brown.
5. Cut each sandwich in half and serve for a snack or appetizer.

Chickpea Patties with Apricot Mayo

MAKES 8 TO 10 SERVINGS

I have made these patties with cooked lentils and flavored them with curry. Vegetarians will enjoy these as their main meal. The patties can also replace other starches and be served on the side with poultry, meat, or seafood.

1. Pulse the chickpeas, bread, onion, jalapeño, garlic, oregano, cumin, pepper, and salt in a food processor until coarsely chopped. Remove half the mixture to a medium-sized bowl.

2. Add the eggs to the mixture in the processor and process until almost smooth. Spoon into the chopped chickpea mixture in the mixing bowl and stir until thoroughly combined. If the mixture seems too stiff (some chickpea brands are drier than others), mix in 1 tablespoon of olive oil.

3. Form the mixture into 8 to 10 patties, ½ inch thick each, and place in a large dish or on a baking tray sprayed with nonfat cooking oil. Drizzle about 1 tablespoon of olive oil over the patties. (If desired, cover with plastic wrap and refrigerate several hours.)

4. Cook on a griddle or large skillet over medium-high heat. Add the patties (four at a time if necessary to avoid crowding) and fry 4 to 5 minutes. Spray the tops with cooking oil or drizzle olive oil around the sides of the skillet, turn, and fry the patties 4 to 5 minutes longer, until nicely browned.

5. Serve with the mayonnaise, lettuce, and tomatoes in the pita pockets or on the English muffins.

---

2 cans chickpeas (15 ounces each), rinsed and drained

4 slices nutty oatmeal or wheat nut bread, torn into small chunks

½ large red onion, sliced

1 jalapeño pepper, seeded and sliced

2 cloves garlic, sliced

1 tablespoon dried oregano

1 teaspoon cumin

½ teaspoon freshly ground black pepper

½ teaspoon salt

2 eggs, beaten, or ½ cup egg substitute

1 tablespoon olive oil, plus 1 for moistening, if needed

Apricot-Basil Mayonnaise (see page 87)

Shredded lettuce

Sliced tomatoes

8 to 10 warm pita pockets or toasted English muffins

SIDES, SAUCES, AND SALSAS

Fruit sauces and salsas add spice and flavor to grilled meats, seafood, and vegetables, and, of course, sweet and saucy toppings for desserts. Salsas and stuffings also make great side dishes or fillings for grilled peaches and nectarines as well as mushrooms, sweet peppers, poultry, pork, and other dishes.

Italian Plum—Red Wine Sauce

Small Italian plums, or sugar plums, are so sweet you don't need much added sugar. If making this sauce with tarter plums, increase the sugar to ½ cup. The black pepper is barely discernible but gives the sauce an extra flavor. Serve over ice cream and other desserts or with chicken and game dishes.

¾ cup Pinot Noir

⅓ cup sugar

¼ teaspoon ground cinnamon

¼ teaspoon ginger

¼ teaspoon freshly ground black pepper

1½ pounds sugar plums, pitted and halved

1. Bring the Pinot Noir, sugar, cinnamon, ginger, and pepper to a boil in a heavy-bottomed, 3-quart saucepan over medium-high heat. Cook, stirring for 2 minutes, or until the sugar dissolves. Add the plums and simmer for 15 minutes, or until tender.

2. Spoon into a blender or food processor and purée. To make a thicker sauce, return the puréed plum mixture to the saucepan and cook over low heat for 10 minutes. Serve at room temperature or refrigerate for up to 1 week.

Fresh Fruit Sauce

MAKES ABOUT 1½ CUPS

This is the fastest and freshest fruit purée you can make; serve it with chicken, pork, and seafood. Add a little honey or sugar to turn it into a sweet, nonfat sauce for ice cream and other desserts.

1 pound ripe apricots or 3 ripe nectarines, peaches, or plumcots

Juice of about ⅓ lemon (1 tablespoon)

2–3 tablespoons fruit juice (orange, apple, raspberry, or other flavor of your choice)

1. Pit the fruits and cut them in quarters.
2. Purée them in a blender with the lemon juice and other fruit juice until smooth.

VARIATION: To make this a dessert sauce, before puréeing, heat the juice, add ¼ cup honey or sugar, and stir until dissolved, about 3 minutes.

Eden Garden's Pluot Sauce

MAKES ABOUT 4 CUPS

Mary Anne Brenkwitz makes this with the Flavor King pluots that her husband, Steve, grows on their Eden Garden farm in Tracy, California. Flavor King sauce is Steve's favorite topping for ice cream. (See the Brenkwitz Family profile on page 14).

2½ pounds pluots, pitted and chopped (4 cups)

1 cup sugar

1 cup water

1. Bring all the ingredients to a boil in a large saucepan over medium-high heat. Cook 10 minutes, stirring constantly, until it reaches a syrupy consistency.
2. Keep refrigerated for up to 1 month.

Fruit Dip Sauce

MAKES ABOUT 1½ CUPS DIP (2 OR 3 SERVINGS)

1 carton (8 ounces) nonfat peach
or vanilla yogurt

1 large ripe plum, plumcot, or
peach, pitted and cut in quarters
(or substitute 1 cup canned or
frozen peach slices)

½ cup pitted dried plums or dried
apricots

2 tablespoons honey

¼ teaspoon ground cinnamon

2–3 cups assorted fresh fruit cut
in chunks or sliced (apricots,
peaches, nectarines, apples,
pears, strawberries, and grapes
work well)

1. Purée the yogurt, plum, dried plums, honey,
   and cinnamon in a blender and pour into two
   small bowls.
2. Place the bowls in the middle of plates and
   surround with the fresh fruit.
3. Serve with cocktail forks or plastic fruit picks
   to spear fruit and swirl in the dip.

Ham and Salsa Pinwheels

MAKES ABOUT 30 PINWHEEL SLICES

*Use the same recipe to make appetizers with
smoked turkey and Apricot-Avocado Salsa
(see page 80).*

4 spinach-flour tortillas,
8 inches each

1 container (4 ounces) nonfat or
low-fat garlic and herb or chive
soft cheese

4–6 ounces thinly sliced ham

¾ cup Minted Plum and Donut
Peach Salsa (see page 78)

1. Spread each tortilla with 2 tablespoons of the
   soft cheese and layer the ham over the top.
   Spoon 3 tablespoons of the salsa over each
   layer of ham.
2. Roll the tortillas tight, jelly-roll style, and
   enclose each in plastic wrap. Refrigerate for
   1 to 6 hours.
3. Remove from the refrigerator 20 minutes
   before serving, remove the plastic, and cut the
   rolls into 1-inch diagonal or straight slices.

Nectarine-Blueberry Salsa

MAKES 4 CUPS

2 large nectarines, pitted and diced

1 cup fresh blueberries

1 cup (2 ears) fresh corn (or substitute frozen or canned)

1 small red onion, diced fine

1 handful of Thai or cinnamon basil leaves, chopped

Juice of 1 medium orange (⅓ to ½ cup)

2 jalapeño peppers, seeded and diced

3 cloves garlic, minced fine

2 tablespoons rice wine vinegar

1 tablespoon olive oil

Freshly ground black pepper

Salt

1. Mix all the ingredients in a serving bowl and allow the flavors to mingle for 1 hour. Season with salt and pepper to taste.
2. Refrigerate for up to 1 week.

Apricot Relish

MAKES ABOUT 3 CUPS

1 pound apricots, pitted and chopped (or substitute one 15-ounce can, drained)

1 red bell pepper, chopped

3 scallions, cut in thin slices

2 tablespoons chopped cilantro leaves

2 tablespoons seasoned rice vinegar

1 tablespoon sweet mirin

¼ teaspoon ground cumin

¼ teaspoon curry powder

1. Combine all ingredients in a mixing bowl. Cover for 1 hour. Serve at room temperature.
2. Keep refrigerated up to 1 week. Use a slotted spoon when using the relish on sandwiches.

Kate Zurschmeide's Peach-Tomato Salsa

MAKES 4 CUPS

Kate is co-owner of Great Country Farms in Bluemont, Virginia.

4–5 medium tomatoes, diced (2 cups)

3 ripe medium peaches, peeled, pitted, and diced (1½ cups)

½ large sweet or red onion, diced (½ cup)

1 clove garlic, minced fine

Juice of 1 lime (2 tablespoons)

1 tablespoon fresh jalapeño pepper, seeded and minced

1 teaspoon sugar

¼ teaspoon salt (or to taste)

1. Combine all the ingredients in a large bowl, cover, and allow the flavors to blend for at least 1 hour.
2. Refrigerate for up to 1 week.

Fried Plantains with Fruit Salsa

MAKES 4 SERVINGS

Julio Fuentes, owner of La Chocita Grill in Leesburg, Virginia, serves these with a secret Peruvian sauce. They taste just as delicious with a fruit salsa.

2 ripe plantains

¼ cup canola oil

⅛ teaspoon salt

Freshly ground black pepper

1. Peel the plantains and cut in long diagonal slices ½ inch thick.
2. Heat the oil in a large skillet over medium-high heat. When the oil sizzles, fry the plantain slices 2 minutes on each side, or until golden. Remove to a cutting board and flatten the slices to a ¼-inch thickness with a spatula.
3. Return the plaintains to the hot oil and fry 2 minutes longer. Drain the slices on paper towels, place on a plate, and add salt and pepper to taste. Serve warm with either of the salsas on page 78.

MICHAEL KRAMER

Executive Chef, McCRADY'S RESTAURANT, Charleston, South Carolina

Located in downtown Charleston, South Carolina, McCrady's is housed in the original brick structure built in 1788 by Edward McCrady. Then called McCrady's Tavern, it was the setting for many of Charleston's early celebrations and musical gatherings, including a dinner party thrown for George Washington in 1791 during his tour of the South. After taking several downturns from tavern to coffeehouse to dilapidated warehouse, the building was finally restored to its former glory in 1982, and is now listed on the National Register of Historic Places and Landmarks.

Since Executive Chef Michael Kramer and his founding partner, Tradd Newton, opened the new McCrady's in 1999, the award-winning cuisine, wines, and service in this charming, upscale tavern are anything but old and stuffy, despite their historic home. As a graduate of the California Culinary Academy in San Francisco, Kramer trained under some of the country's best chefs, including Wolfgang Puck of Spago and Dean Fearing of The Mansion on Turtle Creek in Dallas, where he was discovered by Tradd Newton.

McCrady's has won accolades and awards from the high priests of the food industry, including the *Wine Spectator*'s coveted "Best of" Award of Excellence for 2003. Boasting a wine list of nearly 1,000 selections, McCrady's was one of 139 new restaurants worldwide to receive the award.

The restaurant's menu changes almost weekly to take advantage of fresh seasonal ingredients and as a way to create anticipation for his clientele and keep his skills and those of his staff on the cutting edge of modern-day styles. Kramer blends French-influenced dishes and classic cooking techniques to create what he calls progressive American cuisine. Since he started cooking his goal has been "simple preparations with balanced layers of intense flavors and harmonious colors and textures."

If his menu changes frequently, continuity is found in the tantalizingly fresh-flavored sauces he serves with many of his preparations. Crediting Puck for teaching him about sauces, Kramer says, "I believe it's the sauces that complete the symphony of flavors." His passion for creating levels of textures and flavors is obvious in such dishes as Pan-Roasted Sea Scallops with Leeks and Truffle Butter, Yellowtail Snapper with Artichokes and Truffle Emulsion, and Butter Poached Lobster with Fennel and Broccoli Purée. Spiced grilled tuna is paired with a red wine glaze, an oven-roasted sea bass with chili peppers, and potato gnocchi with chanterelles.

Kramer developed two new dishes for this book — McCrady's Crab Cakes with Peach-Thyme Chutney (page 102) and McCrady's Scallops with Apricot Curry and Cilantro Yogurt (page 104).

Minted Plum and Donut Peach Salsa

MAKES ABOUT 3 CUPS

Juice of ½ lime or ⅓ lemon
(1 tablespoon)

1 tablespoon hot pepper jelly

1 tablespoon olive oil (garlic
flavored preferred)

4 ripe donut peaches or 2 white
peaches, pitted and diced

2 large ripe purple or red plums
or pluots, pitted and diced

½ medium red onion,
chopped fine

1 ripe jalapeño pepper, seeded
and chopped fine

1 medium green bell pepper,
chopped

½ cup mint leaves, chopped

1. Whisk together the lime juice, hot pepper
   jelly, and oil in a large bowl.
2. Stir in the peaches, plums, onion, jalapeño,
   and bell pepper. Cover until ready to serve or
   refrigerate for up to 1 week.

Black Bean–Nectarine Salsa

MAKES 9 CUPS

2 cans black beans (15 ounces
each), rinsed and drained

5 nectarines, pitted and diced
(or substitute 1 can (30 ounces)
sliced peaches, drained)

1 large red bell pepper, diced

4 scallions, thinly sliced

2 cloves garlic, finely chopped
or crushed

⅓ cup snipped fresh cilantro

Juice of 1 lime
(about 2 tablespoons)

Zest of 1 lime
(about 2 teaspoons)

2 teaspoons ground cumin

2 teaspoons dried oregano

½ teaspoon garlic salt

½ teaspoon freshly ground black
pepper

1. Mix all the ingredients in a large bowl and
   allow the flavors to mingle for 1 hour.
2. Refrigerate for up to 1 week.

Apricot-Orange-Cranberry Sauce

MAKES ABOUT **4** CUPS

1 cup dried apricots

Juice of 1 orange (½ cup)
(or substitute commercial)

2 medium oranges, washed
and cut in 8 pieces

1 package (12 ounces)
fresh cranberries

1 cup honey

½ teaspoon ground cinnamon

½ teaspoon ground ginger

*Serve this sauce with roasted or grilled chicken, turkey,
and pork. I like to eat it all by itself for dessert or breakfast.
It's also wonderful stirred into yogurt or spooned over
baked apples and fruit crisps.*

1. Bring the apricots and orange juice to a boil in a small saucepan over high heat. Remove to a medium-sized bowl and set aside to cool.
2. Place the orange pieces in a food processor and roughly chop. Add the apricot mixture, half the cranberries, and the honey, cinnamon, and ginger and process until roughly chopped. Add the remaining cranberries and process until coarsely or finely chopped, as preferred.
3. Spoon the mixture into a bowl, cover, and refrigerate until chilled. If you won't be using the sauce right away, spoon into airtight containers instead and refrigerate for up to 2 weeks. You can also freeze for up to 6 months.

Apricot-Avocado Salsa

When local super-sweet corn is at its peak, add 1 cup of kernels to the recipe (cook the ears for 2 minutes before removing the kernels) and enjoy the burst of crunch and sweetness in every mouthful. This salsa goes particularly well with seafood, whether served on the side or spooned over the top.

1. Mix the apricots, avocados, and onion in a medium serving bowl.
2. Mash together the garlic, lime juice, mayonnaise, dill, and pepper in a small bowl.
3. Using a rubber spatula, stir the dressing into the apricot mixture. Cover with plastic wrap and refrigerate for 1 hour to allow the flavors to mingle. Serve at room temperature.

¾–1 pound ripe apricots or nectarines, pitted and diced

2 medium ripe avocados, peeled, pitted, and cut in ½-inch dice

½ sweet onion, chopped fine (about ½ cup)

1 clove garlic, minced fine

Juice of 2 limes (3–4 tablespoons)

2–4 tablespoons reduced-fat mayonnaise

1 tablespoon snipped fresh dill

¼ teaspoon freshly ground black pepper

Peach-Onion-Chickpea Sauce

1 tablespoon olive oil

1 large sweet onion, sliced

4 cloves garlic, sliced

½ teaspoon freshly ground black pepper (or to taste)

½ teaspoon salt (or to taste)

2 large peaches or nectarines, pitted and sliced (or substitute a 15-ounce can, drained)

1 can (15 ounces) chickpeas or white cannellini beans, drained and rinsed

¼ cup carrot or apple juice

1 teaspoon ground coriander

1 teaspoon ground cumin

½ cup finely chopped flat-leaf parsley

This is a sauce and a dip, so serve it with raw vegetables or as a topping for ravioli, grains, and baked potatoes. Vary the flavor by adding curry, hot peppers, ginger, or lemon and basil, cilantro, or tarragon leaves instead of the parsley.

1. Heat the olive oil in a large skillet over medium-high heat. When hot, add the onion and sauté for 5 minutes, stirring occasionally.

2. Stir in the garlic, pepper, and salt. Sauté for 3 minutes.

3. Add the peaches to the skillet. Cook for 8 to 10 minutes, stirring occasionally. Remove from the heat.

4. Place the chickpeas in a food processor with the juice, coriander, and cumin. Process for 1 minute. Add the peach mixture and process until smooth. The peaches should provide sufficient liquid. However, if the chickpeas are of a dry nature, add more juice or olive oil to produce a thinner consistency.

5. Spoon the mixture into a bowl and stir in the parsley. Taste and adjust the flavor by adding more coriander, salt, or pepper. Serve the sauce hot (reheat in the skillet for 5 minutes), at room temperature, or chilled. This sauce will keep, refrigerated, for up to 1 week.

Tofu-Yogurt-Plum Sauce

MAKES 2 1/2 CUPS

Plums are particularly flavorful for this sauce, but you may also use pluots or plumcots instead, or add an apricot or two. Serve this sauce with grilled swordfish, mackerel, bluefish, pork, or chicken. It can also be used as a dressing, tossed with spinach greens and sliced nectarine, mango, apple, or strawberries.

1. Place the tofu, yogurt, plums, honey, lime juice, curry, and ginger in a blender or food processor and purée until smooth, about 2 minutes.
2. Remove to a serving bowl and stir in the lime zest. Sprinkle the top with the basil.
3. Refrigerate for up to 1 week.

1 cup soft silken tofu

1 cup nonfat vanilla, lime, or lemon yogurt

2 medium-large red plums, pitted and cut in slices

2–3 tablespoons honey

Juice of 1 lime
(about 2 tablespoons)

1 teaspoon mild or hot curry powder or paste (or to taste)

½ teaspoon ground ginger

Zest of 1 lime
(about 2 teaspoons)

2 tablespoons chopped fresh cinnamon basil

Apricot-Mushroom Bulgur

2 tablespoons olive
or canola oil

3 cloves garlic, minced

1 medium carrot, grated

4–5 scallions, sliced

3 ounces (about 6 medium-
sized) brown mushrooms,
chopped

1 cup bulgur

¼ cup chopped dried apricots
or dried plums (prunes)

½ teaspoon freshly ground
black pepper

½ teaspoon salt

2 cups hot vegetable or
chicken broth

½ cup grated Parmesan

½ cup chopped flat-leafed
parsley or sweet basil

½ cup chopped hazelnuts
or walnuts, toasted (see
page 88)

Bulgur is most famous as the main ingredient in Middle Eastern tabbouleh (tabbouli), which is served cold. This recipe is designed to serve hot on the side or stuffed into peaches, sweet peppers, or tomatoes. It's a dish that appeals to most people, especially vegetarians, and for that reason is a great addition to the buffet table. The same recipe can be made with couscous or rice.

1. Heat the oil in a large skillet over medium-high heat. Sauté the garlic, carrot, and scallions for 2 minutes. Add the mushrooms and sauté for 3 minutes. Stir in the bulgur, apricots, pepper, and salt and cook, stirring occasionally, for 2 minutes

2. Lower the heat and pour in 1 cup of the hot broth, stirring until most of the liquid has been absorbed. Stir in the rest of the hot broth and cook about 10 minutes, until most of the liquid has been absorbed. Stir in the Parmesan and parsley. Remove from the heat.

3. When ready to serve, spoon into a dish or fill halved peaches and sprinkle with the toasted nuts.

Peach-Apple Sauce

MAKES ABOUT 5 CUPS

I make this sauce with fresh peaches when they are peaking locally and the first harvests of late-summer apples are coming in. I also make it with frozen or canned peaches, as well as with canned apricots on occasion. And just like plain applesauce, the peach and apricot versions complement roasted or grilled meats and poultry. Serve warm or cold with roast pork, ham, goose, and other meats. Spoon over oatmeal, pancakes, waffles, French toast, and quick breads (see chapter 2 for bread recipes).

4 large sweet apples (Golden Delicious, Gala, and Honeycrisp work well)

5 large peaches or nectarines (or substitute a 30-ounce jar of canned slices, drained)

1 tablespoon apple juice or water (or substitute canned peach juice)

1 teaspoon ground cinnamon

½ teaspoon ground nutmeg

¼ cup honey (optional)

1. Peel, core, and slice the apples and place in a large, heavy-bottomed pan. Pit and slice the peaches and add to the apples, along with the apple juice, cinnamon, and nutmeg.
2. Cover the pot and simmer over low heat for 20 minutes. Remove the lid and simmer 10 minutes longer. Mash with a potato masher or purée in a food processor or blender in two batches. Stir in the honey if a sweeter sauce is desired.
3. Refrigerate for up to 2 weeks; freeze for up to 1 year.

Apricot-Pecan Corn Bread Stuffing

Peach Jalapeño Corn Bread (see page 23) or equivalent purchased corn bread, crumbled into small chunks

½ cup chopped dried apricots

½ cup Microwave Apricot Jam (see page 46)

½ cup vegetable broth

2 tablespoons olive or canola oil, or butter

1 medium-sized red onion, chopped

1 large celery rib, chopped

2 tablespoons chopped lemon balm or lemon thyme leaves

1 tablespoon grated gingerroot, washed and peeled if preferred

½ teaspoon lemon pepper (or to taste)

½ teaspoon salt

½ cup chopped pecans or walnuts

¼ cup egg substitute or 1 egg, beaten

Serve as a side dish or use as a stuffing for vegetables, pork tenderloin, chicken, or turkey.

1. Preheat the oven to 350°F. Put the bread on a baking sheet and bake for 10 to 15 minutes, or until lightly toasted. If serving the stuffing on the side, spray a 2- to 3-quart baking dish with cooking oil spray and set aside.

2. Bring the dried apricots, jam, and vegetable broth to a boil in a small saucepan over high heat. Remove and set aside.

3. Heat the oil in a large skillet over medium-high heat. Sauté the onion, celery, lemon balm, ginger, lemon pepper, and salt for 5 minutes. Stir in the pecans, toasted bread, apricot mixture, and egg substitute.

4. Spoon into the prepared baking dish, cover with foil, and bake for 20 minutes. Remove the foil and bake 15 minutes longer, or until golden.

NOTE: Spoon the filling loosely into the cavity of the bird just before roasting, not the night before. Cold stuffing may not heat up sufficiently in the center to kill any bacteria that may be present. Bacteria thrive at temperatures lower than 160°F.

Brandied Peach Stuffing

Cook this stuffing in a dish and serve on the side or stuff into vegetables, a large roaster chicken, or a small turkey.

1. Preheat the oven to 350°F. Put the bread pieces on a baking sheet and bake for 10 to 15 minutes, until lightly toasted. If serving the stuffing on the side, spray a 2- to 3-quart baking dish with nonfat cooking oil.

2. Cut the peach slices into chunks and place in a medium-sized saucepan with the brandy and ¼ cup of the reserved juice. Bring to a boil over high heat, remove, and set aside.

3. Heat the oil in a large skillet over medium-high heat. Sauté the onion, red pepper, thyme, pepper, and salt for 5 minutes. Add the bread and peach mixture. Add more of the reserved juice as necessary. Stir in the egg substitute.

4. Spoon into the prepared baking dish, cover with foil, and bake for 30 minutes. Remove the foil and bake 15 minutes longer, or until golden brown.

NOTE: Spoon the filling loosely into the cavity of the bird just before roasting, not the night before. Cold stuffing may not heat up sufficiently in the center to kill any bacteria that may be present. Bacteria thrive at temperatures lower than 160°F.

9 large slices nutty oat bread, torn into small pieces (about 4 cups)

2 cups canned peach slices in juice or light syrup, drained and juice reserved

¼ cup peach brandy

2 tablespoons olive or canola oil, or butter

1 medium onion, chopped

1 large red bell pepper, chopped

1 teaspoon dried thyme leaves

½ teaspoon freshly ground black pepper

½ teaspoon salt (or to taste)

¼ cup egg substitute or 1 egg, beaten

Apricot-Basil Mayonnaise

½ cup chopped dried apricots

½ cup boiling water

¼ cup egg substitute

Zest of about ½ lime
(1 teaspoon)

Juice of 2 limes (¼ cup juice)

2 cloves garlic, cut in half

Small handful of sweet Italian
basil leaves (about ½ cup)

¼ teaspoon freshly ground
black pepper

¼ teaspoon salt

¾ cup olive oil

*Use this homemade mayonnaise as a sauce for fish, chicken,
rice, baked potatoes, grilled vegetables, and steamed broccoli
and cauliflower, and the Chickpea Patties on page 70.*

1. Place the apricots in a small bowl and cover with the boiling water.
   Let cool to room temperature. Drain off any water.
2. Process the cooled apricots, egg substitute, lime zest and juice,
   garlic, basil, pepper and salt in a food processor or blender until
   smooth — stop to scrape down the sides of the container once or
   twice as necessary.
3. With the cover on and the processor running, gradually add the
   olive oil in a thin stream through the top passageway and process
   until the mayonnaise is smooth and creamy. Serve at room temperature or chill. Refrigerate for up to 2 weeks.

Plum and Barley Stuffing

Use this recipe to stuff acorn squash, portobello mushrooms (page 99), roast chicken, and whole baked fish, or serve it by itself as a simple side dish.

1. Heat the oil in a large saucepan over medium-high heat. Sauté the barley, onion, and garlic in the oil for 5 minutes.
2. Add the juice, nectar, dried plums, cardamom, ginger, pepper, and salt and bring to a boil.
3. Cover the pan, reduce the heat to low, and simmer for 10 to 15 minutes, or until the barley is just tender and the liquid absorbed.
4. Remove from the heat and stir in the nuts.

2 tablespoons olive oil

1 cup quick-cooking barley

1 large yellow onion, chopped

1 medium clove elephant garlic, cut lengthwise and thinly sliced

1½ cups carrot juice

1 cup apricot or peach nectar

½ cup sliced dried plums (prunes) or dried apricots

½ teaspoon cardamom

½ teaspoon ground ginger

½ teaspoon freshly ground black pepper

½ teaspoon salt

¼ cup chopped fresh parsley

1 cup toasted chopped pecans or sliced almonds (see box)

TOASTING SEEDS AND NUTS

Toasting seeds and nuts develops their flavors and also gives them a crunchy texture. You can do the toasting simply and quickly in a skillet on top of the stove (this is the preferred method for sesame seeds). Place them in a single layer in a heavy-bottomed skillet over medium-high heat. Stir frequently until they are golden and release a pleasant aroma, 2 to 3 minutes. During the last minute, the color changes quickly, so be ready to remove them from the skillet into a dish to cool.

To toast seeds and nuts in the oven, place them in a single layer on a baking sheet and bake at 350°F for 8 minutes, stirring frequently until golden and fragrant.

ENTRÉES

Apricots, peaches, nectarines, and plums are winning fruits to include in just about any dish imaginable. While they are associated with a raft of mouthwatering desserts, their textures and flavors beg to be used in savory dishes. Depending on which fruit you choose, you can add sweet-tart, all sweet, or tart-sweet accents.

Apricot-Soy-Glazed Ham

MAKES 12–16 SERVINGS

This is such a good company or holiday dish. For a really big crowd, buy a 10-to 12-pound ready-cut spiraled ham so you don't have to do so much slicing. Serve with Apricot-Orange-Cranberry Sauce (see page 79) and you'll have no last-minute preparations to think about.

1. Preheat the oven to 325°F. Score the surface of the ham with shallow diagonal cuts in a diamond pattern, 1 inch apart. Place the ham in a shallow roasting pan and insert a meat thermometer into the thickest part.
2. Bake about 3⅓ hours, or until the meat thermometer registers 145°F. (Count on 20 to 25 minutes per pound.)
3. Meanwhile, mix the apricot chutney, orange juice, soy sauce, mustard, cinnamon, and ginger in a small bowl to make the glaze.
4. After the ham has been cooking for 30 minutes, spoon ¼ cup of the glaze over the ham. During the last 30 and 15 minutes of cooking time, spoon 2 to 4 tablespoons of glaze over the ham again. Remove the ham from the oven and let stand 10 to 15 minutes before cutting into thin slices.
5. Serve with the chutney on the side.

10- to 12-pound spiraled ham

½ cup apricot or peach chutney, such as Apricot-Prune Chutney (see page 44) or McCrady's Peach-Thyme Chutney (see page 103)

¼ cup orange juice

¼ cup reduced-sodium soy sauce

2 tablespoons mustard

½ teaspoon ground cinnamon

½ teaspoon ground ginger

Chicken Peach Satay

MAKES 4-6 ENTRÉES OR 18 HORS D'OEUVRES

3 firm peaches or nectarines, pitted, cut in quarters, then cut again in 3 pieces, for a total of 36 chunks

2 pounds boneless, skinless chicken breasts, cut into ¼-inch-thick strips

1 large sweet onion, cut into 18 squares (1 inch each)

½ cup peach nectar or water

¾ cup chunky peanut butter

2 tablespoons honey

2 cloves garlic, crushed

¼ cup reduced-sodium soy sauce

3 tablespoons seasoned rice vinegar or juice of 1½ limes (about 3 tablespoons)

2 tablespoons roasted sesame oil

1 teaspoon hot sesame or chili oil

1 teaspoon grated gingerroot or ground ginger

Traditionally, satay is served on bamboo skewers. To prevent scorching, soak 18 skewers (8 inches each) in cold water for 30 minutes before using. Instead of serving as appetizers, prepare these as the main meal and serve with jasmine or basmati rice. If preferred, substitute pork or beef tenderloin for the chicken and plums for the peaches.

1. Preheat the grill if you plan to cook these as soon as you've made them. Otherwise, they can be refrigerated after preparation.
2. Tightly thread the skewers with two chunks of peach alternated with several strips of chicken, ending with one piece of onion. Lay the skewers in a shallow pan or on a baking tray.
3. Heat the nectar in a small saucepan over medium heat. When warm, remove and stir in the peanut butter, honey, and garlic. When mixed, stir in the soy sauce, vinegar, sesame oil, hot oil, and ginger.
4. Spoon about ¼ cup of the satay sauce over the skewered chicken. (Reserve the remaining sauce to serve with the grilled kabobs.) If you don't plan to cook the kabobs right away, cover and refrigerate. Otherwise, proceed.
5. Grill directly over medium-high heat (or oven-broil 4 inches from heat) 5 minutes on each side.
6. Serve three or four skewers per person and provide individual bowls for the dipping sauce.

Peach-Apple Sauce Turkey Meatloaf or Burgers

MAKES 6 SERVINGS

This mixture will make 6 burgers or one meatloaf. Serve the meatloaf or the burgers with more Peach-Apple Sauce, Plum-Apple Chutney (see page 54), Barbecue Sauce (see page 53), or Any-Fruit Ketchup (see page 53).

1. Preheat the oven to 350°F. Spray a 9- by 4-inch loaf pan with cooking oil spray.
2. Combine the bread crumbs, onion, ½ cup of the sauce, turkey, egg substitute, mustard, dried herbs, Worcestershire, pepper, and salt in a large mixing bowl. Use a large fork or your hands and mix thoroughly.
3. Spoon into the loaf pan and bake for 45 minutes. Spoon the remaining ½ cup of sauce over the top and bake 20 minutes longer.
4. If making turkey burgers, panfry or grill and serve between slices of toasted or grilled ciabatta bread.

Cooking oil spray

2 large slices whole wheat bread, toasted and processed into coarse crumbs, or 1 cup commercial bread crumbs

½ red onion, chopped fine

1 cup Peach-Apple Sauce (see page 84)

1½ pounds ground turkey

¼ cup egg substitute or 1 egg, beaten

2 tablespoons mustard

1 tablespoon mixed dried herbs (thyme, oregano, rosemary, basil)

2 teaspoons Worcestershire sauce

½ teaspoon freshly ground black pepper

¼ teaspoon salt

Ciabatta bread (optional; use if making burgers)

Baked Salmon Steaks with Apricot-Orange-Cranberry Sauce and Wild Rice

MAKES 4 SERVINGS

¼ cup chopped parsley

2 cloves garlic, minced

3 tablespoons olive oil or melted butter

Juice of about ⅔ lemon (2 tablespoons)

½ teaspoon freshly ground black pepper

½ teaspoon salt

4 salmon steaks

Apricot-Orange-Cranberry Sauce (see page 79)

2 cups cooked hot wild rice

My brother enjoys cooking but nothing too complicated, thank you. He makes his home with my mother in Scotland, and cooks this simple recipe for them once a week. My mother pulls out one of her homemade chutneys to serve with the salmon steaks. I find the Apricot-Orange-Cranberry Sauce a refreshing accompaniment.

1. Preheat the oven to 350°F.
2. Combine the parsley, garlic, oil, lemon juice, pepper, and salt in a shallow baking dish. Add the salmon steaks and turn to coat evenly with the liquid.
3. Cover the dish with foil and bake for 20 minutes. Remove the foil and bake 5 minutes longer, or until the salmon flakes easily.
4. Accompany each serving with 2 tablespoons of the relish and pass the rest at the table to spoon over the wild rice. If desired, also stir ¼ cup of the sauce into the rice before serving.

Grilled Tuna with Plum-Peach Salsa

MAKES 4 SERVINGS

You may also cook the tuna on top of the stove in a large cast-iron or other thick-bottomed skillet over high heat. Sear the tuna steaks for 2 minutes per side for rare and 3 minutes for medium-rare.

1. Mix the sesame oil, soy sauce, garlic, ginger, and pepper in a small bowl. Pour half the marinade into a rectangular dish, place the tuna steaks on top, and cover with the remaining marinade. Cover the dish with plastic wrap and refrigerate 4 to 24 hours or leave at room temperature for 30 minutes to 1 hour.

2. Preheat the grill to high. Position the rack no more than 4 inches from the flame or briquettes.

3. Drizzle the tuna with 2 tablespoons of the olive oil. Flip the steaks and drizzle with the rest of the olive oil.

4. Place the tuna on the rack. For rare tuna, grill for 2 to 3 minutes per side. For medium-rare tuna, grill 3 to 4 minutes per side. Before turning the steaks to grill the second side, spoon the marinade over the top. Continue cooking to desired doneness.

5. Roll the hot steaks in the toasted sesame seeds and place on individual plates on top of the salad greens. Spoon ¼ cup of the plum-peach salsa on each plate and pass the rest at the table.

¼ cup sesame oil

¼ cup sesame soy sauce

1 clove garlic, minced

1 teaspoon grated gingerroot

½ teaspoon freshly ground black pepper

4 tuna steaks, 1 inch thick each

¼ cup olive oil

¼ cup toasted sesame seeds (See Toasting Seeds and Nuts, page 88)

6–8 cups mixed Asian or spring salad greens

2 cups Minted Plum and Donut Peach Salsa (see page 78), substituting cilantro for the mint

Grilled Halibut with Nectarine Salsa

Juice of about 4 limes (⅓ cup)

2 tablespoons sweet mirin or honey

2 tablespoons garlic-flavored olive oil

2 rcd jalapeño peppers, seeded and quartered

1 tablespoon fresh tarragon leaves or ¼ cup cilantro leaves

1½ pounds halibut, cut into four servings

1 tablespoon olive oil

½ teaspoon salt

¼ teaspoon freshly ground black pepper

2 bunches watercress, washed and tough stems removed

Nectarine-Blueberry-Salsa (see page 75) or Apricot-Avocado Salsa (see page 80)

Serve with rice, couscous, or barley and Nectarine-Blueberry Salsa or Apricot-Avocado Salsa.

1. Pulse the lime juice, mirin, garlic-flavored olive oil, jalapeños, and tarragon in a blender for 20 seconds until smooth.
2. Pour half of the marinade into a baking dish, add the halibut pieces, and pour the remaining marinade over the top. Cover and marinate for at least 30 minutes at room temperature. Alternatively, marinate in the refrigerator for several hours and bring to room temperature during the last 30 minutes.
3. Preheat the grill.
4. Remove the halibut from the marinade. Bring the marinade to a boil in a small saucepan; reduce the heat and simmer for 5 minutes. Remove from the heat and cool.
5. Place the halibut on a plate with the olive oil, salt, and pepper. Turn to coat each side with the oil.
6. Grill over medium heat for 5 minutes; turn and cook 5 minutes longer, until the flesh flakes easily. (Or broil or panfry the halibut for 4 minutes per side, until the flesh flakes easily.)
7. Place on individual plates. Spoon the salsa over the watercress and serve on the side. Pass the jalapeño marinade separately at the table.

Swordfish with Nectarines and Olives

Swordfish can be dry. Immersing the steaks in lemon juice helps to tenderize them. Serve with couscous or rice.

1. Mix the water, lemon juice, and sea salt in a rectangular dish. Place the swordfish in the liquid (if they are not covered with liquid, add a drop more water) and soak 10 minutes.

2. Meanwhile, prepare the marinade. Mix the peach nectar, mint, parsley, and sweet and hot paprika in a pitcher or small bowl.

3. Drain the swordfish and lay on paper towels. Discard the salt water and pour the nectar marinade into the dish. Add the swordfish and turn each side a couple of times in the marinade. Set aside.

4. Heat the olive oil in a large, deep heavy skillet over medium-high heat. Sauté the onions, garlic, and the pepper about 3 minutes.

5. Add the nectarines to the skillet and toss the ingredients together. Sprinkle ¾ cup of the olives over the top.

6. Remove the swordfish from the marinade and arrange in a single layer on top of the onion mixture. Pour over the marinade and top with the remaining ¾ cup of olives.

7. Cover the skillet, reduce the heat to low, and simmer for 30 minutes, or until the swordfish is tender. A good way to serve this dish is over salad greens: Layer the onion-nectarine mixture first and top with the swordfish. Drizzle with any remaining pan juices.

1½ cups water

Juice of 2 lemons (¼ cup)

1 tablespoon sea salt

4 swordfish steaks, 1 inch thick each

½ cup peach nectar

¼ cup chopped mint leaves

¼ cup chopped flat-leaf parsley

2 tablespoons sweet paprika

1 teaspoon hot paprika

3 tablespoons olive oil

2 medium-large red onions, halved and cut into thin slices

4 cloves garlic, minced

1 teaspoon freshly ground black pepper

4 nectarines, pitted and sliced ½ inch thick (or one 16-ounce can sliced peaches, drained)

1½ cups pitted black olives, cut in half

Shrimp-Fruit Stir-Fry with Noodles

2 tablespoons olive
or canola oil

4 scallions, sliced

4 teaspoons minced garlic

2 teaspoons grated gingerroot

1½ pounds fresh or frozen
medium shrimp, shelled and
deveined

½ teaspoon McCormick's
Spicy Season-All or salt-free
Mrs. Dash Original Seasoning
Blend

1 nectarine, pitted and diced

1 red plum, pitted and diced

½ cup sliced strawberries or
diced kiwi

1 tablespoon roasted dark
sesame oil

¼ teaspoon freshly ground
black pepper

¼ teaspoon salt

2 cups vegetable or chicken
broth

8 ounces bean thread noodles
(¼ inch wide)

The fruit gives this dish a natural sweetness.

1. Heat 1 tablespoon of the oil in a large heavy wok or skillet over medium-high heat. Sauté the scallions, 2 teaspoons of the garlic, and 1 teaspoon of the gingerroot for 1 minute.
2. Turn the heat to high and pour the remaining oil around the sides of the skillet. Add the shrimp, stirring to mix with the scallions and garlic. Sprinkle with the Season-All and stir-fry for 3 minutes, turning the shrimp so that both sides hit the heat.
3. Add the nectarine, plum, and strawberries to the skillet and stir to mix. Reduce the heat to low, cover the skillet, and cook for 3 minutes. Remove the shrimp and fruit to a bowl with the juices.
4. Heat the sesame oil in the skillet over medium-high heat and add the remaining garlic and ginger. Stir-fry 1 minute. Add the pepper, salt, and vegetable broth and bring to a boil. Drop the noodles into the broth and cook for 4 minutes, or until tender.
5. Return the shrimp and fruit to the skillet and stir to combine. Serve immediately or at room temperature.

Baked Trout with Plum Sauce

Cooking oil spray

¼ cup olive oil

1 teaspoon ground five-spice powder

½ teaspoon freshly ground black pepper

1 clove garlic, minced

2 scallions, cut in thin slices

4 rainbow trout or 8 large fillets, heads removed

Oriental Plum Sauce

1. Preheat the oven to 400°F. Spray a baking tray with cooking oil spray.
2. Mix the olive oil, five-spice powder, pepper, garlic, and scallions and spoon into the cavity of each trout.
3. Bake 15 minutes, or until the flesh down the backbone flakes easily.
4. Skin the trout and remove the bones before serving.
5. Drizzle the (boned) fillets with the Oriental Plum Sauce.

Oriental Plum Sauce

MAKES ABOUT 4 CUPS

2 pounds ripe red or purple plums, pitted and cut in wedges

¼ cup honey

1 tablespoon grated gingerroot

1 tablespoon water

3 cloves garlic, chopped

½ teaspoon red chili paste (or to taste)

¼ cup reduced-sodium soy sauce

1. Bring the plums, honey, ginger, water, garlic, and chili paste to a boil in a medium-sized heavy pan over high heat.
2. Reduce the heat to low and simmer for 15 minutes, or until the plums are soft. Remove from the heat and stir in the soy sauce.
3. Ladle the plum mixture into a food processor or blender and purée.
4. Refrigerate for up to 1 week. Alternatively, pour into airtight containers, leaving a ½-inch headspace, and freeze up to 1 year.

Wendy's Stuffed Portobello Mushrooms

Cooking oil spray

¼ cup homemade
or commercial basil pesto

4 large (6-inch) portobello
mushrooms, stems removed
and skin peeled, if necessary

1 tablespoon olive oil,
garlic-flavored if possible

2 tablespoons balsamic
vinegar or red wine

Plum and Barley Stuffing
(see page 88)

My vegetarian daughter, Wendy, regularly makes these mushrooms for a main meal. When they are stuffed with barley, couscous, or corn bread stuffing, they are a hearty side dish and all that you need to serve with an entrée of fish, tofu, beef, or chicken.

1. Spray a large skillet with cooking oil spray and place over medium heat. Spread 1 tablespoon of the pesto inside each portobello cap and arrange them skin-side down in the skillet. Drizzle the oil around the edges of the skillet, cover, and cook for 5 minutes.

2. Remove the cover, add the balsamic vinegar to the skillet, and cook 5 minutes longer. Reduce the heat and cook 5 minutes longer, or until the portobellos are tender.

3. Place on individual plates and spoon any pan juices over the top. Heap the Plum and Barley Stuffing over each. (Alternatively, use another stuffing or rice dish.)

Teriyaki Salmon Fillet with Peaches

This is one of my favorite ways to cook salmon — it is always flavorful and moist. Served with sautéed peaches and couscous or rice, it makes a fast week-day dinner an easy company dish. Sometimes I grill the salmon with halved peaches or nectarines (see Grilling and Broiling on page 103).

½ cup store-bought sesame-ginger sauce

¼ cup orange juice

¼ cup teriyaki sauce

2 tablespoons roasted sesame oil

1½ pounds salmon fillet, skin removed

1 teaspoon olive oil

½ teaspoon freshly ground black pepper

4 medium-sized peaches, pitted and sliced, or one can (16 ounces) peach slices, drained

Cooking oil spray

Small handful of snipped basil or cilantro leaves

4 cups Asian salad greens

1. Mix the sesame-ginger sauce, orange juice, teriyaki sauce, and sesame oil in a shallow dish. Add the salmon and marinate at room temperature for 30 minutes or in the refrigerator for several hours (bring to room temperature before cooking).

2. Heat the olive oil and pepper in a large skillet over medium heat. Add the sliced peaches and cook for 5 minutes. Turn off the heat.

3. Spray a large nonstick skillet with cooking oil spray and place over medium heat for 1 to 2 minutes. Remove the salmon from the marinade, place dark side down in the hot skillet, and sear for 2 minutes.

4. Pour the marinade into the skillet and sprinkle the basil leaves over the top. Cook for 5 minutes.

5. Turn the fillet, reduce the heat to low, and cook 4 to 5 minutes longer, or until it is no longer (or barely) translucent in the center.

6. Remove the cooked salmon from the skillet and cut into four servings. Place over a bed of greens, spoon the peaches over the top, and drizzle with the warm teriyaki sauce from the skillet.

Shrimp and Scallop Kabobs with Grilled Plums

½ cup low-fat coconut milk

1 tablespoon fish sauce

Zest of 1 lime (2 teaspoons)

1 teaspoon chopped canned red chiles or red chile paste

3 cloves garlic, minced

2 pickled umeboshe plums, minced

Small handful of basil leaves, chopped (Siam Queen, cinnamon, or lemon)

¾ pound fresh or frozen large scallops

¾ pound fresh or frozen medium-sized shrimp, peeled and deveined

4 large firm plums, cut in half, pits removed

It's easy to grill the fruit at the same time you grill the kabobs. Use fresh pluots when they are in season; they are a special treat with the seafood. I serve this dish with basmati rice cooked with ½ cup of low-fat coconut milk to replace some of the cooking water.

1. Mix the coconut milk, fish sauce, lime zest, chile, garlic, umeboshe plums, and basil in a long rectangular dish. Add the scallops and shrimp and toss to mix with the marinade. Cover and refrigerate for at least 30 minutes and up to several hours.

2. Preheat the grill.

3. Thread the scallops and shrimp on four skewers, each 12 inches long. Place the kabobs and the plums over medium heat on the grill, brush all with the marinade, and grill 5 minutes. Turn; brush again with the marinade and grill 5 minutes longer.

4. Bring any remaining marinade to a boil in a small saucepan; reduce the heat and simmer 5 minutes. Remove from the heat and let cool to room temperature. Pour over the cooked kabobs.

VARIATION: You may also broil the kabobs. Place them on a rack set in a baking pan and broil 4 inches from the heat for 3 to 4 minutes. Turn and broil 4 minutes longer. Brush with the marinade as outlined above. Broil or roast the plums as recommended in Grilling, and Broiling on page 103 or Roasting Fruit on page 109.

McCrady's Crab Cakes with Peach-Thyme Chutney

MAKES 4 SERVINGS

Michael Kramer, executive chef and co-owner of McCrady's Restaurant (see the profile on page 77) in Charleston, South Carolina, is right in the middle of southern peach country. South Carolina is the second (albeit a far second) most important peach-growing region in the United States. California leads in all stone fruit production, growing 90 percent of the country's peaches.

1. Mix the crab, ¾ cup of the bread crumbs, and the mayonnaise, lemon juice, cilantro, and scallions in a large mixing bowl. Season with the salt and pepper to taste.

2. Form the mixture into eight cakes (2-ounce portions) and coat in the remaining bread crumbs. Refrigerate for 20 to 30 minutes while making the chutney.

3. Preheat the oven to 400°F. Pour the oil into a large (13-inch), deep skillet and heat to 350°F over medium-high heat using a thermometer.

4. Place the crab cakes in the hot oil and cook for 2 minutes. Flip and cook 5 minutes longer, or until golden brown. Remove from the oil with a slotted spatula and place on a baking tray. Bake 5 minutes to finish.

5. Place two crab cakes on each plate and serve with the chutney.

1 pound jumbo lump crabmeat, picked

1½ cups bread crumbs

¾ cup reduced-fat mayonnaise

Juice of about ⅔ lemon (2 tablespoons)

1 tablespoon cilantro, finely chopped

1 tablespoon thinly sliced scallions

Salt and freshly ground black pepper

½ cup canola oil

McCrady's Peach-Thyme Chutney (see opposite page)

McCrady's Peach-Thyme Chutney

MAKES 2 CUPS

1 tablespoon butter

3 peaches, peeled, pitted, and cut into ¼-inch dice

¼ cup firmly packed brown sugar

¼ cup white wine

1 tablespoon finely chopped fresh thyme leaves

This chutney sauce is the companion for McCrady's Crab Cakes (see opposite page), and any other dish that calls for chutney.

1. Brown the butter slightly in a medium sauté pan over medium heat. Mix the peaches with the butter.
2. Add the sugar and stir for 2 minutes, until melted.
3. When the sugar has formed a glaze over the peaches, add the white wine and cook 4 to 5 minutes, or until a syrup forms.
4. Sprinkle with the chopped thyme. Cook, stirring, 1 minute longer. Remove from the heat.
5. Purée ½ cup of the chutney in a blender. Pour the purée back into the pan with the remaining chutney and cool.
6. Refrigerate for up to 1 week, if desired.

GRILLING AND BROILING

Cut the fruits in half, remove the pits, and spray with butter-flavored oil or olive oil or brush with marinade. Place skin-side up on a hot grill or skin-side down under a broiler and cook for 3 to 4 minutes. Turn the fruits with a metal spatula and grill or broil the other side for 3 minutes, or until tender. Firm-ripe fruits work best for grilling.

McCrady's Scallops with Apricot Curry and Cilantro Yogurt

MAKES 4 SERVING

Executive chef Michael Kramer has created a scallop dish that is a masterpiece of wonderful flavors and food styling. Make it once and you will make it many times, especially to wow dinner guests when you set down the plates.

1. Heat the oil in a large, deep skillet over high heat.
2. Season the scallops generously with the salt and pepper to taste.
3. When the oil is hot, add the scallops to the saucepan and sear for 2 minutes on both sides. Reduce the heat to low and cook for 5 minutes longer, or until the scallops are opaque in the center. Remove from the oil with a slotted spatula and place on a warm plate (lined with paper towels, if desired).
4. Pour the apricot curry in a circle in the center of four plates. Drizzle the cilantro yogurt around the edges of the curry. Place the sea scallops on top of the curry and serve.

½ cup canola oil

12 large deep sea scallops

Salt and freshly ground black pepper

McCrady's Apricot Curry (see opposite page)

McCrady's Cilantro Yogurt (see opposite page)

McCrady's Apricot Curry

MAKES 2 CUPS

This sauce is great with fish, meat, or poultry.

2 cups dried apricots

½ small onion, chopped

1 lemongrass stalk

2 teaspoons Madras curry powder

½ teaspoon fennel seed, toasted

1 bay leaf

4 cups water

Salt and freshly ground black pepper

1. Bring the apricots, onion, lemongrass, curry powder, fennel seed, bay leaf, and water to a boil in a large saucepan over medium heat. Reduce the heat to low and simmer 5 to 10 minutes, or until the liquid is reduced by half and the apricots are tender.
2. Discard the lemongrass and bay leaf. Pour mixture in a blender, purée until smooth; season with the salt and pepper to taste.
3. Refrigerate for up to 1 week, if desired.

McCrady's Cilantro Yogurt

MAKES 1½ CUPS

This flavored yogurt is ideal for any broiled or grilled fish and vegetables.

1 bunch cilantro

1 cup plain nonfat yogurt

Salt and freshly ground black pepper

1. Blanch the bunch of cilantro in boiling water for 10 seconds; immediately plunge into ice water.
2. Place the cilantro, water clinging to the leaves, in a blender and purée until smooth, adding a little ice water if necessary. Press the purée through a fine strainer.
3. Add the yogurt and season with the salt and pepper to taste.
4. Refrigerate for up to 1 week, if desired.

McCrady's Plum Sauce

This is a wonderful sauce to have on hand. Use it as a salad dressing, with grilled tuna or pork chops, or McCrady's Crab Cakes on page 102.

1. Bring the plums, wine, mirin, lemongrass, shallots, and ginger to a boil in a medium-sized saucepan over medium heat. Reduce the heat to low and simmer 20 minutes, until the liquid is reduced by three quarters. Remove the lemongrass.
2. Add the scallions to the plum mixture. Purée in a blender.
3. Press the purée through a fine strainer into the saucepan or a bowl. Stir in the black sesame seeds and season with the salt and pepper to taste.

8 medium-sized red plums, pitted and sliced

2 cups plum wine

1 cup aji mirin

1 lemongrass stalk

2 large shallots, thinly sliced

1 teaspoon grated gingerroot

6 scallions, white part only

1 teaspoon black sesame seeds

Salt and freshly ground black pepper

ASIAN INGREDIENTS

Miso paste is thick and available in white, yellow, and red. Made from soybeans and grains, it is a staple in Japanese kitchens, where it is used to flavor soups, dipping sauces, meats, and dressings. Look for it in the refrigerated section of Asian food markets, health food stores, and large supermarkets.

Mirin is seasoned sweet rice wine (*aji mirin* is salted and sweet) and can be found in Asian food markets or the specialty sections of larger supermarkets.

Umeboshi pickled plums and *Ume plum vinegar* can usually be found sharing a shelf in Asian food markets or health food stores.

Grilled Beef Tenderloin with Elephant Garlic and Nectarines

⅓ cup prepared Dijon mustard or jalapeño mustard

¼ cup snipped chives

2 tablespoons olive oil

6 beef tenderloin steaks, cut 1 Inch thick

2–3 whole heads elephant garlic, skins removed (allow 2 cloves per person)

6 nectarines, cut in half and pitted

Olive oil spray

Salt and freshly ground black pepper

Grilled elephant garlic is nutty and sweet. If you want the garlic to be soft enough to spread on the steaks or on bread, then you will want to roast it (see Roasting Elephant Garlic below). Serve with hot or cold potato salad.

1. Preheat the grill to medium heat.
2. Mix the mustard, chives, and oil in a shallow dish. Roll the steaks in the mixture to coat on all sides.
3. Place the garlic cloves and nectarines in a dish and spray with olive oil spray.
4. Arrange the steaks, peaches, and garlic on the grill directly above the heat. Sprinkle with the salt and pepper to taste. Grill 4 to 6 minutes per side for medium-rare, 2 minutes longer per side for medium-well, or 4 minutes longer per side for well done. Watch the peaches carefully so they don't burn.
5. Place the steaks, peaches, and garlic on individual plates. Pass the potato salad separately at the table.

ROASTING ELEPHANT GARLIC

Preheat the oven to 350°F. Arrange the whole heads of garlic in a baking dish, drizzle with olive oil to coat (or spray with olive oil spray), and bake for 45 minutes, or until soft. Cool and snip off the tops. Scoop out the soft garlic with a small spoon or split the loose skins and remove the soft flesh from each clove by squeezing it.

Rosemary-Marinated Roast Chicken with Fruit Stuffing

MAKES 4–6 SERVINGS

For flavor, economy, and ease of cooking, it's hard to beat a whole roasted chicken. Cooking the stuffing on the side makes it even easier because you can prepare it while the chicken is roasting. Choose a stuffing and cook it as a side dish or stuff the bird with it — you can do either with this recipe.

1. Mix the peach nectar, soy sauce, oil, shallot, and rosemary in a small bowl.
2. Place the chicken in a large pan and pour half the marinade into the cavity and the rest over the top. Lift the chicken so the marinade runs underneath. Cover the pan and refrigerate 6 to 12 hours, turning the chicken on each side for 2 hours, if possible. Alternatively, place the chicken and marinade in a roasting bag and turn it over two or three times.
3. Preheat the oven to 450°F. Remove the chicken from the marinade and place in a large roasting pan, reserving the marinade for later. Season the chicken with the pepper. If stuffing the chicken, spoon the stuffing into the cavity now. Otherwise, bake the stuffing separately according to the individual recipe directions. (Stuffed or not, I do not truss the chicken — tie its legs together.)

(continued on facing page)

1¼ cups peach or apricot nectar

⅓ cup reduced-sodium soy sauce

3 tablespoons garlic-flavored olive oil

1 large shallot, chopped fine (about ¼ cup)

1 tablespoon fresh rosemary leaves, chopped (or substitute 1½ teaspoons dried rosemary)

1 whole chicken (5–6 pounds)

½ teaspoon freshly ground black pepper

Stuffing of your choice (try Brandied Peach Stuffing on page 86)

4. Roast the chicken in the oven for 20 minutes. Reduce the oven to 400°F and baste the chicken with ¼ cup of the reserved marinade. Discard any leftover marinade. Loosely tent the chicken breast with aluminum foil.

5. Continue roasting the chicken for 45 minutes, basting with the sauce another two or three times. Remove the foil and bake 30 minutes longer.

6. Test to see if the chicken is done by slitting the skin inside the leg thigh (next to the rib cage). If the flesh is too pink, make a longer slit in the skin to slightly expose the uncooked meat. Do the same with the other leg. Baste the chicken with the pan juices and continue to roast for 10 to 15 minutes longer.

7. When the chicken is no longer pink, the juices run clear, and the drumsticks move easily, it is done. Transfer to a serving platter or a carving board and let rest 10 minutes before carving.

8. While the chicken is resting, pour the pan juices into a fat separator. Discard the fat and pour the fat-free juices into a pitcher to accompany the chicken. Or add the juices to your usual chicken gravy.

ROASTING FRUIT

Cut the fruits in half, remove the pits, and place in a single layer, cut-side up, in a baking dish that is sprayed with butter-flavored oil or olive oil. Sprinkle the fruits with ¼ to ½ cup of sugar flavored with ½ teaspoon of ground cinnamon and drizzle with 3 to 4 tablespoons of melted butter. Or spray with butter-flavored oil and drizzle with 2 tablespoons of peach or apricot nectar or apple juice. If a more savory flavor is desired to accompany a robust entrée, eliminate the butter and sugar and drizzle with ¼ cup of honey teriyaki sauce. Cover the dish with foil and bake at 400°F for 10 minutes. Remove the foil and bake for 10 to 15 minutes longer, or until the fruit has softened and caramelized. Place under the broiler for 2 minutes if you prefer a more caramelized finish.

Roasted Turkey with Apricot-Pineapple Sauce

MAKES 8–10 SERVINGS

Roasting whole turkey breast is like having your cake and eating it too. It cuts cooking time in half, you still get pan juices for gravy, and there are breast leftovers for sandwiches.

1. Mix the nectar, preserves, soy sauce, pineapple, ½ teaspoon pepper, garlic salt, ginger, and cinnamon in a medium saucepan. Cook over medium heat for about 2 minutes, until the preserves have melted. Remove from the heat and set aside.

2. Preheat the oven to 400°F. Remove excess fat from the turkey breast and place in a roasting pan sprayed with cooking oil spray. Rub the olive oil all over the skin side of the breast and season with ground pepper to taste. Insert a meat thermometer into the thickest part of the turkey breast, but not where it will touch bone.

3. Reduce the heat to 350°F and roast the turkey in the oven for 30 minutes. Baste with 2 to 4 tablespoons of the apricot-pineapple sauce every 30 minutes until done. The turkey is done as soon as the thermometer registers 175°F, about 2 hours.

4. Remove the turkey breast from the oven, place on a board, and let rest 10 to 15 minutes before carving.

5. In the meantime, pour the pan drippings into a fat separator. Pour the fat-free juices into the remaining apricot-pineapple sauce and heat until warm. Carve the turkey breast and pass the sauce at table.

½ cup apricot nectar

¼ cup apricot preserves, such as Microwave Apricot Jam (see page 46)

¼ cup reduced-sodium soy sauce

1 can (15¼ ounces) crushed pineapple in juice

½ teaspoon freshly ground black pepper, plus more to taste

½ teaspoon garlic salt

½ teaspoon ground ginger

¼ teaspoon ground cinnamon

1 bone-in turkey breast, 5–6 pounds (if frozen, thaw 48 hours in the refrigerator)

Cooking oil spray

1 tablespoon olive oil

Flank Steak with Peaches

Flank steak is an extremely flavorful cut of meat. When grilled quickly, it is also very tender. It always garners rave reviews — whether marinated for 1 or 24 hours. A longer marinating time, however, really does it justice.

½ cup red wine

½ cup peach nectar

¼ cup reduced-sodium soy sauce

2 tablespoons roasted dark sesame oil

1 nectarine or peach, pitted and sliced

3 cloves garlic, cut in half

1 inch gingerroot, washed (peeled if preferred) and sliced

1 flank steak, 1½ pounds, ¾–1 inch thick

2 tablespoons olive oil

Grilled Vegetables and Peaches (optional, see page 103 for grilling instructions)

1. Pulse the red wine, nectar, soy sauce, sesame oil, nectarine, garlic, and ginger in a blender or food processor for 20 seconds. Pour into a 9- by 11-inch baking dish, add the flank, and turn two or three times to coat each side thoroughly. Cover the dish and marinate for 1 to 24 hours in the refrigerator, turning two or three times in the marinade. Remove the flank from the refrigerator and bring to room temperature for 30 minutes.

2. While the flank is coming to room temperature, preheat the grill to medium. If you are grilling vegetables and fruit do so now. Place in a dish, cover with aluminum foil, and keep warm on the side of the grill. Increase the heat to high.

3. Pour off and reserve the marinade from the flank steak. Pour 2 tablespoons of olive oil over the flank and turn to coat. Place on the grill directly over the heat.

4. Baste with the reserved marinade and grill 4 minutes on each side for medium rare, 5 to 7 minutes on each side for medium well.

5. Let stand 5 minutes before cutting widthwise into thin slices with a sharp knife held at a 45-degree angle.

Grilled Turkey Breast with Chili Pluots

MAKES 8–10 SERVINGS

1. Preheat a covered grill to medium hot. Arrange the coals around a drip pan. On a gas-fired grill, set the drip pan between the two burners.

2. Mix the jam, 2 tablespoons olive oil, mustard, black pepper, chili powder, cumin, salt, and cayenne in a small saucepan. Cook over medium heat for about 2 minutes, until the jam is melted.

3. Remove excess fat from the turkey and spread the mustard mixture on the top, back, and sides of the turkey breast. Insert a meat thermometer into the thickest part of the turkey breast, but not where it will touch bone.

4. Place the turkey breast skin-side down on the grill rack, directly over the heat. Lower the hood and cook 20 minutes. Move the turkey away from the direct heat and position over the drip pan. Lower the hood again and cook until the thermometer registers 175°F, about 1¾ hours. (Add more coals, if necessary, to maintain the heat.)

5. To make the chili pluots, heat the olive oil in a large saucepan over medium heat. Cook the shallots and chili powder for 2 minutes. Add the sugar and vinegar and cook for 2 minutes, until the sugar has melted. Stir in the pluots. Reduce the heat to low, cover, and simmer for 10 minutes. Remove from the heat and set aside.

6. Remove the turkey breast from the grill, place on a board, and let rest 10 to 15 minutes before carving. Serve with the chili pluots.

¼ cup plum jam

2 tablespoons olive oil

1 tablespoon mustard

½ teaspoon freshly ground black pepper

½ teaspoon chili powder

½ teaspoon ground cumin

½ teaspoon salt

⅛ teaspoon cayenne pepper

1 bone-in turkey breast, 5–6 pounds (if frozen, thaw 48 hours in the refrigerator)

Chile Pluots

1 tablespoon olive oil

2 large shallots, chopped

½ teaspoon chili powder

¼ cup firmly packed brown sugar

¼ cup balsamic vinegar

6 medium-large ripe pluots or red or black plums, pitted and chopped

Bishop's Split Roast Chicken with Roasted Potatoes and Pickled Peaches

MAKES 4 SERVINGS

4 russet or other large potatoes, peeled and cut into 1-inch slices

1 head of garlic, cloves peeled

Salt and freshly ground black pepper

¼ cup plus 1 tablespoon olive or vegetable oil

1 whole chicken, 4 pounds, split in half

2 sprigs fresh thyme (or to taste), chopped

2 teaspoons coarse sea salt, or to taste

1 teaspoon ground sweet paprika, or to taste

Simply Bishop's Pickled Peaches (see page 44)

When I read this recipe in Simply Bishop's, *it reminded me of my mother's chicken stovies — chicken layered over potatoes and cooked on top of the stove. This oven-roasted dish, however, has much more flavor.*

1. Preheat the oven to 375°F.
2. Place potato rounds and garlic cloves in a roasting pan and season with the salt and pepper to taste. Add the oil and toss until the potatoes are evenly coated.
3. Arrange the potato rounds flat in the pan and surround with the garlic cloves. Lay the chicken halves, skin-side up, on top of the potatoes. Brush the chicken with the remaining 1 tablespoon of oil and season with the thyme, sea salt, and paprika.
4. Cover loosely with a sheet of aluminum foil, shiny-side in, and roast in the oven about 1½ hours. The chicken should no longer be pink, the juices should run clear, and the drumsticks should move easily. Remove the chicken from the roasting pan and wrap in the aluminum foil to keep warm.
5. Return potatoes and garlic to the oven to brown, about 15 minutes.
6. Carve the chicken and arrange the slices on plates with two or three potato rounds each. Serve with the peaches.

Bishop's Roast Pork Tenderloin with Apricot and Sage Stuffing

MAKES 4–6 SERVINGS

Bishop's Restaurant in Vancouver serves this with roasted apples or pears. Roasted nectarines or plums, however, are also delicious served alongside.

1. Preheat the oven to 400°F. Trim the fat and silver skin from the tenderloin.
2. Use a sharp knife to butterfly the pork by making a long deep cut down the length, being sure not to cut right through. Open the tenderloin and pound it lightly to flatten. Season the inside with the salt and pepper to taste.
3. Mix the sausage, apricot, and sage in a bowl and spread the mixture inside the flattened tenderloin. Fold over to partially enclose the stuffing. Use butcher's twine to tie the tenderloin closed in four places. Rub with the olive oil and season with more salt and pepper to taste. Insert a meat thermometer in the center.
4. Place the tenderloin cut-side up in a roasting pan. Roast for 45 minutes or until the internal temperature reads 160°F.
5. Remove from the oven and allow the pork to rest in a warm place, uncovered, for 15 minutes before carving.
6. Carve the pork into 1-inch slices and place on warm plates. Garnish with the sage leaves.

1½ pounds pork tenderloin

Salt and freshly ground black pepper

½ pound pork sausage

2 tablespoons finely chopped dried apricot

1 tablespoon chopped fresh sage leaves

1 tablespoon olive oil

12 small sage leaves for garnish

Grilled Pork Tenderloin with Nectarine-Blueberry Salsa

2 cloves garlic, minced

Zest of about ½ orange
(2 teaspoons)

2 jalapeño peppers, seeded
and minced

1½ tablespoons olive
or canola oil

1½ pounds pork tenderloin

2 tablespoons honey or
jalapeño jelly

¼ cup orange juice

Nectarine-Blueberry Salsa
(see page 75)

Depending on the size and thickness of the tenderloin, I often grill directly over heat. That means dispensing with a drip pan. If you do this, you will want to place newspapers beneath the grill to catch the drips.

1. Preheat a covered grill to medium hot. Arrange the medium-hot coals around a drip pan. On a gas-fired grill, set the drip pan between the two burners.

2. Mix the garlic, zest, peppers, and oil in a small bowl.

3. Trim any fat from the tenderloin and spoon the garlic oil mixture over the top. To avoid too much contact with the peppers, wear gloves to rub the mixture all over the tenderloin.

4. Insert a meat thermometer into the center of the pork and place on the grill over the drip pan. Cover and cook for about 1 hour.

5. During the last 15 minutes, mix together the honey and orange juice and use to baste the pork. Remove from the grill when the thermometer registers 160°F. There should be no more pink and the juices should run clear.

6. Let the pork rest 10 minutes before carving into slices. Arrange on plates and spoon the salsa on top.

Thai Peanut—Plum Pork Chops

MAKES 4 SERVINGS

If using canned plums in light syrup, add 2 tablespoons of mirin at first and taste for sweetness.

1. Place the fresh plums in a medium-sized saucepan with the water, cover, and simmer 15 minutes, until soft. Remove from heat and let plums cool. Place in a blender or food processor with the mirin, onion, and peanut sauce mix and purée until smooth.

2. Place the chops in a dish and spread each side with 1 tablespoon of the purée. Reserve the remaining purée.

3. The chops can be refrigerated for several hours at this point or cooked without delay. If refrigerating, bring the chops to room temperature for about 30 minutes before grilling or broiling.

4. To grill, preheat the grill to medium. Lightly brush or spray the grill with nonfat cooking oil. Grill 7 to 10 minutes per side, until the juices run clear and the center is slightly pink. Don't overcook, or the chops will be tough. Test after 7 minutes by slicing into the center of one chop with a small, sharp knife.

5. To broil, preheat the oven to broil. Place pork on the rack of a broiler pan positioned 4 inches from the heat. Broil 8 minutes per side, or until the juices run clear and the center is slightly pink.

6. Pour the reserved plum purée into a saucepan and bring to a boil. Reduce the heat and simmer 2 minutes or so. Spoon over the chops or pour into a pitcher.

4 large ripe plums, pitted and cut into chunks (or substitute one 15-ounce can of plums in juice)

¼ cup water

¼ cup sweet mirin

½ small red onion, cut in 4 pieces

1 packet (1 cup) Thai peanut sauce mix (there are usually two envelopes in a packet containing ½ cup each)

4 boneless pork loin chops, 1 inch thick

Note: Substitute peaches or apricots (fresh, frozen, or canned) for the plums, if you wish. The flavor is not as intense, but the sauce is equally delicious.

Pork Chops with Salsa

1 cup peach nectar

½ cup teriyaki sauce

Juice of about 1½ limes
(3 tablespoons)

2 tablespoons mustard

1 teaspoon grated ginger

1 tablespoon roasted dark
sesame oil

Small handful of cinnamon
basil or cilantro leaves

4 boneless pork loin chops,
1 inch thick

Black Bean–Nectarine Salsa
(see page 78)

*The salsa will provide a hearty side of beans and vegetables,
eliminating the need for other dishes.*

1. Mix the peach nectar, teriyaki sauce, lime juice, mustard, sesame oil, and basil in a small bowl. Place the chops in a dish or gallon-sized, heavy-duty sealable plastic bag. Pour ½ cup of the marinade over the chops and cover the dish with plastic wrap or seal the bag firmly. Refrigerate the remaining marinade.
2. Marinate in the refrigerator for 1 to 24 hours, turning the chops at least once. Bring the chops to room temperature for about 30 minutes before grilling or broiling. Remove the pork chops from the marinade.
3. Preheat the grill to medium (if grilling) or the oven to broil (if broiling).
4. To grill, place the chops directly over the heat on a grill rack lightly brushed or sprayed with oil. Cook 7 to10 minutes on each side, until the juices run clear and the center is slightly pink. Don't overcook or the chops will be tough. Test after 7 minutes by slicing into the center of one chop with a small, sharp knife.
5. To broil, place the chops on the rack of a broiler pan positioned 4 inches from the heat. Broil 8 minutes on each side, or until the juices run clear and the center is slightly pink.
6. Heat the reserved marinade and serve with the chops. Accompany with the salsa.

Sesame Tofu, Spinach, and Plum Stir-Fry

Don't use silken tofu for this recipe; the texture is too soft. Use firm tofu packed in water. If a chewier, meatier texture is preferred, freeze the tofu first. When thawed, slice blocks in two horizontally, place between paper towels, and press. Change paper towels until all liquid has been removed. Do the same with refrigerated tofu. To give slices a crunchy coating, dip in egg substitute and then in flour before stir-frying.

1 pound firm or extra firm tofu, cut in 1- by 2-inch slices

½ cup peach or apricot nectar

½ cup teriyaki sauce

4 cloves garlic, minced

1 piece fresh ginger 2 inches long, grated or minced (or use a combination of shredded garlic and ginger, available in jars in Asian markets)

¼ cup sesame seeds

2 tablespoons roasted dark sesame oil

4 red plums, pitted and cut into ½-inch chunks

¼ cup chopped fresh chives or scallion greens

1 pound young spinach leaves

½ teaspoon freshly ground black pepper (or to taste)

1. Place the tofu in a single layer in a dish. Mix the nectar, teriyaki sauce, garlic, and ginger and pour over the tofu. Marinate 30 minutes at room temperature or in the refrigerator for 1 to 24 hours. Remove the tofu from the marinade and place on paper towels. Reserve the marinade.

2. Toast the sesame seeds in a large skillet over medium-high heat for 1 minute, stirring constantly. Remove to a plate.

3. Increase the heat to high, pour the sesame oil into the skillet, and, when hot, add the tofu slices. Sauté 2 to 3 minutes on each side, or until browned and heated through. Remove and toss with the toasted sesame seeds.

4. Add 2 tablespoons of the reserved marinade to the skillet and sauté the plums for 3 to 5 minutes. Add the rest of the marinade and the chives, spinach, and pepper. Stir-fry 2 minutes to wilt the spinach. Divide the plum-spinach mixture among four plates and top with the sautéed tofu and sesame seeds.

SHAKES, SMOOTHIES, AND BEVERAGES

Packed with fresh vitamins and nutrients, they can be whipped together in about five minutes flat for a fast and healthy breakfast, a quick lunch, or an afternoon snack. There are other kinds of drinks that benefit from juicy fruits as well. Peach and apricot nectars are delicious additions to iced teas, sparkling soda drinks, and even cocktails.

Breakfast of Champions Shake

MAKES ABOUT 6 CUPS (4 SERVINGS)

3 large nectarines, sliced
(or substitute 2 cups canned
peach slices)

1 medium banana, sliced

1½ cups low-fat or nonfat milk
or vanilla soy milk

1 cup low-fat or nonfat yogurt (vanilla,
lemon, or any other fruit flavor)

2–4 tablespoons honey

2 tablespoons low-fat creamy
peanut butter

2 single-serving packets instant oatmeal
(French vanilla, apple-cinnamon, or other
flavor of your choice)

Purée all of the ingredients in a blender until smooth and serve in chilled glasses.

Apricot-Blueberry Shake

MAKES ABOUT 3½ CUPS (2 OR 3 SERVINGS)

If the dried apricots are hard, soak in ½ cup of hot water for about 15 minutes.

2 cups low-fat vanilla soy milk

1 cup fresh or frozen blueberries

8 ounces soft silken tofu

¼ teaspoon ground ginger
or cinnamon

2 tablespoons vanilla soy protein powder
(available in pharmacies, health stores,
and some supermarkets)

Purée all of the ingredients in a blender until smooth, serve immediately.

Peach, Banana, and Berry Soy Milk Smoothie

MAKES ABOUT 6 CUPS (4 SERVINGS)

2 cups low-fat vanilla soy milk

1 cup peach applesauce

1 cup peach or apricot nectar

1 cup frozen strawberries or blueberries

2 medium bananas, sliced

2–4 tablespoons honey

¼ cup vanilla soy protein powder (available in pharmacies, health stores, and some supermarkets)

Crushed ice (optional)

1. Purée all of the ingredients in a blender until smooth.
2. Serve over crushed ice.

Apricot-Strawberry Smoothie

MAKES ABOUT 3 CUPS (2 SERVINGS)

4 large apricots, pitted and quartered (or substitute one 15-ounce can)

1½ cups frozen strawberries

1 cup nonfat milk (or substitute soy milk or rice milk)

½ cup apricot nectar or canned apricot juice

1 medium banana, sliced

Purée all of the ingredients in a blender until smooth and serve.

HOW MANY IN A POUND?

The number of plums in 1 pound varies among the varieties. Japanese plums, for example, range in size from very large to small-medium with the result that there may be as few as 4 and as many as 12 in 1 pound.

Apple, Apricot, and Cantaloupe Smoothie

MAKES ABOUT 4 CUPS (3 OR 4 SERVINGS)

1 large sweet apple (Gala, Honeycrisp, and Golden Delicious work well), cored and chopped

1 can (15 ounces) apricot halves in juice or light syrup

1 cup cantaloupe or watermelon chunks

1 cup crushed ice

½ cup apple juice

2–4 tablespoons honey

Purée all of the ingredients in a blender until smooth and serve.

Nectarine and Blueberry Yogurt Smoothie

MAKES ABOUT 5 CUPS (4 SERVINGS)

3 large nectarines or peaches, pitted and quartered (or substitute 2 cups canned or frozen slices)

2 cups peach or vanilla ice cream

1 cup low-fat or nonfat blueberry yogurt, semi-frozen (for semi-frozen, place in the freezer for 15 to 20 minutes)

1 cup nonfat milk

⅛ teaspoon cinnamon

1. Purée all of the ingredients in a blender until smooth.
2. Pour into chilled glasses and serve immediately or refrigerate until chilled to your liking.

Just Peachy Shake

MAKES ABOUT 4¹/₂ CUPS (3 SERVINGS)

3 juicy peaches, pitted and quartered
(or substitute 2 cups canned slices)

2 tablespoons honey

1 cup peach applesauce

1 cup peach nectar or apple juice
(or substitute juice or syrup from
canned peaches, if using)

1 cup low-fat or nonfat peach, apricot,
or vanilla yogurt, semi-frozen (for semi-
frozen, freeze 15 to 20 minutes)

Crushed ice (optional)

1. Purée all of the ingredients in a blender until smooth.
2. Serve over crushed ice (if using).

Mango-Plum Shake

MAKES ABOUT 4¹/₂ CUPS (3 SERVINGS)

1 mango, peeled and sliced

4 large plums or pluots, sliced

1 cup low-fat or nonfat milk

1 cup lemon sorbet or frozen yogurt

Purée all of the ingredients in a blender until smooth and serve in chilled glasses.

PEELING EASILY

An easy way to peel these fruits is to plunge them into boiling water for no more than 20 seconds. Remove and place in ice-cold water. The skins should slip off quite easily. If not, using a small paring knife, start at the stem end and pull off the skin.

To stop the flesh from turning brown, dip in a solution of 1 tablespoon lemon or lime juice to 1 quart water, or simply sprinkle with lemon or lime juice.

White Peach Cream Soda

If you've ever had an egg cream (which doesn't include eggs), you'll see that this is a takeoff. Use chocolate syrup if you wish.

3 ripe white peaches or nectarines, pitted and sliced (or substitute 2 cups canned slices)

1½ cups nonfat milk

¼ cup vanilla syrup

12-ounce bottle cream soda

1. Purée the peaches, milk, and vanilla syrup in a blender or food processor until smooth.
2. Pour into four glasses and top each with cream soda. Stir to blend.

Apricot-Raspberry Tea

MAKES 6 SERVINGS

You could also try these ingredients to make tea: lemon tea with peach nectar and fresh mint; black currant tea with peach nectar and lime; mint tea with apricot nectar.

4 cups hot water

4 raspberry tea bags

3 cups apricot nectar, chilled

1 cup ice cubes

6 packets sugar substitute (such as Equal) or 3 tablespoons superfine sugar (or to taste)

1 lemon, sliced

1. Pour the hot water over the tea bags and steep for 5 minutes.
2. Discard the bags and freeze the tea for 15 to 20 minutes, to chill.
3. Pour the tea and the chilled nectar into a pitcher over the ice and stir in the sugar substitute. Serve with the lemon slices.

Earl Grey Apricot Cocktail

MAKES 2 SERVINGS

Make this into a nonalcoholic tea by increasing the apricot nectar to ¾ cup and eliminating the apricot brandy.

½ cup crushed ice

½ cup apricot nectar

1 cup cold Earl Grey tea

¼ cup apricot brandy

2 long strips of lime zest, for garnish

1. Place two glasses in the freezer for 10 minutes. Remove the glasses and scoop the crushed ice into them.
2. Pour the nectar and tea into the glasses and top with the brandy. Stir.
3. Garnish with the lime zest.

Cranberry-Peach Surprise

MAKES 1 SERVING

Use raspberry or orange juice, if preferred.

½ cup cranberry juice

¼ cup peach brandy

2 tablespoons crushed ice

1. Pour the juice and brandy over the ice.
2. Stir and enjoy.

Vodka Nectar

MAKES 1 SERVING

Add a splash of tonic water if you wish.

¼ **cup vodka**

½ **cup peach or apricot nectar**

2 **tablespoons crushed ice**

Pour the vodka and nectar over the crushed ice and stir.

FROZEN FRUIT FOR SMOOTHIES AND SHAKES

Instead of using crushed ice to make smoothies and shakes, add frozen fruits to the blender and the flavor will be much richer. It's a good idea to keep a bag of sliced peaches and other sliced fruits or berries in the freezer just for that purpose. It's easy to slice and freeze your own fruits (see pages 40–42). This also goes for bananas, which give a thick, creamy quality to blended concoctions. But don't wait until the bananas are too ripe. Choose those that are bright yellow with barely any flecks of brown on the skin — these have a bigger flavor and creamier flesh. Place peeled and sliced bananas and other fruits in a single layer in plastic freezer bags, and use as needed.

Nectarine-Rum Limeade

MAKES 4 SERVINGS

Make this into a drink to share with young ones by substituting peach nectar for the hard liquor.

2 **cups peach-flavored seltzer or mineral water**

3 **ripe nectarines, pitted and sliced (or substitute 2 cups canned or frozen slices)**

1 **cup white rum or gin**

Juice of 4 limes (½ cup)

½ **cup crushed ice**

8 **packets sugar substitute (such as Equal) or ¼ cup superfine sugar**

4 **sprigs of mint**

1. Combine the seltzer, nectarines, rum and lime juice in a blender and puree until smooth. Add the ice and sugar to taste and liquify.

2. Divide the limeade into 4 glasses and garnish with a sprig of mint.

DESSERTS

Even if we can't get to an orchard, chances are, whether in a big city or a country village, there are farmers' markets selling baskets of tree-ripened fruits. So take a few pounds home to eat fresh but also to turn into delectable pies, tarts, crisps, cakes, kuchens, sherbets, and ice creams. In fact, add them to any dessert that will be enhanced by their flavor and moisture.

White Nectarines with Strawberry Cream

If you prefer, instead of making a cream with mascarpone or soft tofu, mash fresh strawberries or raspberries into 1 quart of vanilla ice cream.

1. Toss the nectarines with the strawberries and sugar in a dessert dish or individual dessert bowls or goblets.
2. Beat together the mascarpone, cream, vanilla, confectioners' sugar, and crushed strawberries in a medium bowl.
3. Spoon the strawberry cream over the nectarines. Cover and refrigerate, if desired.

3 large ripe white nectarines or peaches, pitted and sliced

2 cups sliced strawberries

3 tablespoons sugar

1 cup mascarpone or soft tofu

¼ cup light cream or vanilla soy milk

1 teaspoon vanilla extract

¼ cup confectioners' sugar

½ cup fresh or frozen strawberries, crushed

White Peach Melba with Raspberries

Auguste Escoffier, the greatest French chef of all time, created this peach dish for Nellie Melba, the Australian soprano. Here, white peaches are substituted for the traditional yellow.

Divide the ice cream among six dishes, spoon the peach halves on top, fill with the raspberries, and drizzle with the liqueur.

1 quart vanilla ice cream,

3 large ripe white peaches peeled, halved, pitted, and poached (see page 151)

1½ cups fresh raspberries

6 tablespoons peach or raspberry liqueur

Roasted Peaches Stuffed with Dried Fruits

Butter-flavored cooking oil spray

1 cup peach or apricot nectar

¼ cup dried cranberries

2 tablespoons snipped dried plums

¼ cup chopped walnuts or pecans

2 tablespoons firmly packed light brown sugar

¼ teaspoon ground cardamom

¼ teaspoon ground nutmeg

4 large peaches or nectarines, halved and pitted

1 cup nonfat vanilla yogurt

These stuffed peaches (or nectarines or large plums) make a light and delicious dessert that tastes even more glorious with a creamy nonfat vanilla yogurt spooned over the top.

1. Preheat the oven to 350°F. Spray an 8-inch square or 9-inch round baking dish with butter-flavored cooking oil spray.
2. Combine the nectar, dried cranberries, and dried plums in a small saucepan. Bring to a boil, remove from the heat, and let stand for 5 minutes. Drain the nectar and reserve in a small pitcher.
3. Stir the walnuts, sugar, cardamom, and nutmeg into the fruit mixture.
4. Place the peach halves in the baking dish and spoon the fruit mixture into the center of each peach. Pour the reserved nectar over the top of the fruits.
5. Bake 20 to 25 minutes, spooning pan juices over the peaches halfway through. Serve warm with pan juice and the yogurt spooned over the top.

Plum Sherbet

When plum season is over, use canned plums plus the juice and reduce the buttermilk by ½ cup.

1½ pounds ripe plums or pluots, pitted and sliced

Juice of ½ lemon (1 tablespoon)

3 cups low-fat buttermilk, chilled

1¼ cups sugar (¼ cup less if using sweetened canned plums)

½ teaspoon ground cinnamon

¼ cup liquid egg white substitute or 2 egg whites, beaten

1. Purée the plums, lemon juice, and ½ cup of the buttermilk in a blender or food processor.
2. Add the remaining buttermilk and the sugar, cinnamon, and egg white substitute and blend together. Refrigerate for 1 hour.
3. Pour into an ice-cream maker and freeze according to the instructions for your brand.

Peach Ice Cream

MAKES 12 SERVINGS

Though classic ice-cream recipes call for a base of egg custard, this easy recipe is thickened with sweetened condensed milk.

1½ pounds (3–4) ripe peaches, peeled, pitted, and sliced (or 3 cups canned or frozen slices)

½ cup sugar

1 tablespoon peach brandy or vanilla extract

2 cups half-and-half cream, chilled

1 cup low-fat milk, evaporated milk, or vanilla soy milk, chilled

1 can (14 ounces) sweetened condensed milk, chilled

1. Crush the peaches in a large bowl with a potato masher, to make about 2 cups.
2. Add the sugar and brandy and let stand for 30 minutes, stirring occasionally, until the sugar has dissolved.
3. Add the cream, milk, and condensed milk and stir to mix. Pour into an ice-cream maker and freeze according to the instructions.

Nectarine-Cranberry Sorbet

1½ cups cranberry or cran-raspberry juice

½ cup sugar

2 pounds (4 to 5) ripe nectarines, pitted and sliced (or substitute 4 cups canned slices)

Juice of ⅓ lemon (1 tablespoon)

2 tablespoons liquid egg white substitute or 1 egg white, beaten

Try using orange, mango-orange, or tangerine juice with peaches or plums for a variation on this recipe. Increase the sugar by ¼ cup or to taste when using plums.

1. Combine the juice and sugar in a medium-sized saucepan over medium-high heat. Bring to a boil, stirring until the sugar is completely dissolved.
2. Add the nectarines and lemon juice to the syrup, cover the pan, and cook for 10 minutes. Remove from the heat and let cool 20 to 30 minutes.
3. Purée until smooth in a blender or food processor. Pour into a mixing bowl and incorporate the egg white substitute.
4. Refrigerate for at least 2 hours, then freeze in an ice-cream maker according to the instructions for your brand.
5. Alternatively, pour into a 9- by 13-inch baking dish, cover with plastic wrap, and freeze (in the freezer) until firm, about 2 hours. Spoon into a large bowl and beat with an electric beater on low speed for 1 minute, until the mixture turns to slush. Pour back into the dish, cover with plastic wrap, and freeze (in the freezer) 30 minutes, or until almost solid. Scrape into a mixing bowl, beat with an electric beater as before, return to the dish, cover, and freeze for 2 hours, or until firm.
6. Hard-frozen sorbet is best when left at room temperature for 30 minutes before serving.

Peaches in Caramel Sauce

This is a wonderful topping for ice cream, cake, or dessert pancakes. It's also a great filling for prebaked crusts.

4 tablespoons butter (½ stick)

2 pounds (5–6) peaches or nectarines, pitted and sliced (or substitute 4 cups canned or frozen slices)

1½ cups firmly packed brown sugar

Juice of 1 lime (2 tablespoons)

2 tablespoons rum

1. Melt the butter in a large skillet over medium heat. Add the peach slices and sauté them for 5 minutes.
2. Add the brown sugar, stirring until it has melted and the sauce is bubbling. Add the rum and lime juice and sauté for 5 minutes longer. Cool before spooning into a baked tart crust, if appropriate.

Apricot Rice Pudding

My mother grates fresh nutmeg over the top of this pudding for flavor.

2 quarts whole milk or vanilla soy milk

1 cup chopped dried apricots, soaked in hot water to cover

½ cup uncooked white rice

½ cup sugar

1 tablespoon butter, diced (optional)

1 teaspoon fresh grated or ground nutmeg

1. Preheat the oven to 325°F. Place a 3-quart baking dish on a baking sheet set up next to the oven.
2. Mix the milk, apricots, rice, sugar, and butter (if using) in the dish and sprinkle the nutmeg over the top.
3. Carefully place the baking sheet in the middle of the oven. Bake 1½ hours, or until the top has formed a golden brown crust.

Bishop's Poached Peaches or Apricots

Bishop's uses herb teas in place of water in several recipes. They are a very tasty poaching liquid for fresh fruit.

2 cups water

1 cup sugar

2 bags raspberry tea

1 pound peaches, peeled, or apricots
(no need to peel apricots)

1. Place the water and sugar in a saucepan and bring to a boil over high heat. Remove from the heat and add the tea bags. Allow to steep for 30 minutes before removing the bags.
2. Cut the peaches in half and remove the pits.
3. Bring the syrup to a boil over medium heat. Add the peaches, reduce the heat to low, and simmer until the peaches are tender, about 15 minutes.
4. Remove from the heat and cool. Serve the fruit chilled with the tisane syrup. (Fruit and syrup can be refrigerated for up to 1 week.)

Coconut Cinnamon Crisps

Serve these with roasted, poached, or grilled fruits, and ice cream.

8 egg roll wrappers (6 inches square), cut in half diagonally (or substitute 8-inch flour tortillas, quartered)

1 tablespoon butter, melted, or butter-flavored cooking spray

¼ cup shredded coconut

2 tablespoons sugar

1 teaspoon ground cinnamon

1. Preheat the oven to 400°F.
2. Place the halved egg roll wrappers on a baking sheet. Brush each side with the melted butter.
3. Mix the coconut, sugar, and cinnamon and sprinkle over both sides of the wrappers.
4. Bake 4 to 5 minutes, or until crisp and golden. Remove the baking sheet to a wire rack and cool the crisps.

Italian Prune Plum Tart

MAKES 6-8 SERVINGS

Italian prune plums are sweet and firm and they make a wonderful pie filling. Bake them without a pastry crust and they will taste just as delicious served warm on their own. This recipe includes no spices, but you can always stir ½ teaspoon ground cinnamon, ground ginger, or ground nutmeg (or a combination) into the sugar for additional flavor.

1½ pounds prune plums, split and pitted

1 unbaked crust for a 9- or 10-inch tart (see page 164)

½ cup firmly packed brown sugar

2 tablespoons butter, diced

1. Preheat the oven to 350°F.
2. Going from outside to center, overlap the prune plum halves in the prepared crust.
3. Sprinkle with the sugar and dot with the butter. Bake in the oven for 40 minutes, or until golden and bubbling.

OVEN SPILLS FROM JUICY FRUITS

When baking fruit crisps, crumbles, cobblers, pies, and tarts, it's always a good idea to place the baking dish on a baking sheet to catch any juice that might bubble over. In fact, line the baking sheet with foil and that will make spills even easier to clean up.

Plum and Apricot Cupcakes

1 cup brown sugar

½ cup (1 stick) butter, softened

½ cup egg substitute or 2 eggs, beaten

Juice of ½ orange (2 tablespoons)

Zest of about ¼ orange (1 teaspoon)

1 cup snipped dried apricots

2 large plums, pitted and chopped

2 cups sifted, all-purpose flour

1 teaspoon baking powder

1 teaspoon baking soda

1 teaspoon ground cinnamon

Use dried plums (for additional sweetness) instead of dried apricots, which can be tart, if the plums aren't very ripe. Substitute nectarines or other seasonal stone fruits for the plums.

1. Preheat the oven to 350°F. Line muffin trays with 36 paper liners.
2. Beat the sugar and butter in a large bowl with an electric beater for 2 minutes, until creamy. Beat in the egg substitute, orange juice, and zest. Stir in the apricots and plums.
3. Sift the flour, baking powder, baking soda, and cinnamon into the batter and stir to mix.
4. Spoon into the paper cups to fill halfway and bake 20 minutes, or until a toothpick inserted in the center comes out clean.
5. Remove cupcakes with the liners from the muffin trays and cool on wire racks.

Peach and Apricot Bars

MAKES 12–16 BARS

Cut these into 2-inch squares for a fruity lunch-box treat or into a more generous size for an afternoon snack.

1. Preheat the oven to 350°F. Spray an 8-inch square baking dish with cooking oil spray.
2. Cream together the sugar, butter, and eggs in a large bowl with an electric beater.
3. Mix the flour, cinnamon, baking powder, and baking soda in a separate bowl and stir ½ cup at a time into the egg mixture.
4. Fold the peaches and apricots into the batter.
5. Stir in the walnuts.
6. Spoon the batter into the baking dish. Bake for 30 to 40 minutes, or until a toothpick inserted in the center comes out clean. Cool in the pan on a wire rack. Slice into bars or squares when cool.

Cooking oil spray

¾ cup firmly packed brown sugar

½ cup (1 stick) butter, softened

2 eggs or ½ cup egg substitute

1 cup sifted all-purpose flour

1½ teaspoons ground cinnamon

½ teaspoon baking powder

½ teaspoon baking soda

2 large ripe peaches, halved, pitted, and diced

1 cup chopped dried apricots

½ cup chopped walnuts

Pluot and Cherry Slump

1½ pounds pluots or large sweet purple or red plums, pitted and sliced

½ pound sweet cherries, pitted

½ cup sugar

Zest of ⅔ lemon (2 teaspoons)

1 cup all-purpose flour

1 teaspoon baking powder

¼ cup firmly packed brown sugar

¼ cup (½ stick) butter, sliced and chilled

½ cup milk

Juice of ⅓ lemon (1 tablespoon)

The colonial names for dishes were descriptive of how they looked or sounded during or after cooking. New England slumps were also called grunts on Cape Cod, but baked fruit desserts with a similar sweet dumpling dough topping were known as cobblers in other parts of the country. Serve this slump with vanilla yogurt or ice cream.

1. Preheat the oven to 400°F.
2. Combine the pluots, cherries, sugar, and zest in a medium-sized saucepan. Cover and cook over low heat for 5 to 10 minutes to soften the fruit.
3. Sift the flour and baking power into a medium-sized bowl and stir in the brown sugar. Cut in the butter with a pastry blender or knife until the mixture forms large crumbs.
4. Stir the milk and lemon juice into the flour mixture until just blended.
5. Pour the hot pluot mixture into a 9- by 7-inch (2-quart) baking dish and spoon the dough in dollops over the top.
6. Bake for 30 minutes, or until the crust is golden. Serve warm with the juices from the baking dish.

Seasonal Crisp with Mixed Stone Fruits

Choose your own flavors with whatever fruits are in season: Combine peaches and plums, apricots and nectarines, apricots and plumcots, peaches and cherries, or any two stone fruits. Serve with yogurt, custard, or sour cream sweetened with honey.

1. Preheat the oven to 375°F.
2. Mix the flour, brown sugar, cinnamon, ginger, and nutmeg in a medium-sized mixing bowl. Cut in the butter with a pastry blender or knife until the mixture forms large crumbs.
3. Toss the fruits with the granulated sugar in a 2½-to 3-quart baking dish and spoon the flour mixture over the top.
4. Bake in the middle of the oven for 40 minutes, or until golden.

1 cup sifted all-purpose flour

½ cup firmly packed brown sugar

½ teaspoon ground cinnamon

½ teaspoon ground ginger

½ teaspoon ground nutmeg

6 tablespoons butter, sliced and chilled

3 pounds stone fruits of your choice, pitted and sliced (about 6 cups sliced)

½ cup granulated sugar

Black-Amber Tapioca Pudding

Paul Buxman, of Sweet Home Ranch, California, offers this simple recipe:

"Slice and cook five or six large plums with ⅛ cup water till soft and dark red. Reduce heat, add sugar to taste and two tablespoons of quick-cooking minute tapioca. Stir continuously as it thickens. When tapioca becomes transparent, turn off heat, cover, and let stand for ten minutes. Serve with vanilla yogurt or ice cream."

Apricot–Chocolate Chunk Cookies

MAKES ABOUT 60 COOKIES

Little bites of apricot are a perfect foil for the creamy sweetness of the white chocolate and the bittersweet dark chunks.

1 cup firmly packed brown sugar

1 cup (2 sticks) butter

1½ teaspoons vanilla extract

1 teaspoon baking soda

2 eggs

2½ cups all-purpose flour

6 ounces bittersweet chocolate, cut into chunks

6 ounces solid white chocolate, cut into chunks

½ cup chopped dried apricots

1. Preheat the oven to 375°F.
2. Beat the sugar, butter, vanilla, baking soda, and eggs in a large bowl with an electric mixer until creamy. Add the flour 1 cup at a time, stirring the last half-cup into the mixture by hand, along with the chocolate chunks and apricots.
3. Spoon rounded teaspoons of the dough 2 inches apart on ungreased baking sheets.
4. Place the baking sheets in the middle of the oven and bake 8 to 9 minutes, or until the cookies are lightly golden. Baking longer will produce crisp cookies. Transfer the cookies to a wire rack to cool.

Peach-Almond Crisp

MAKES 6–8 SERVINGS

½ cup sliced almonds

½ cup firmly packed dark brown sugar

½ cup granola

½ cup rolled oats

4 tablespoons (½ stick) butter, melted

1 teaspoon almond extract

2 pounds (5–6) peaches or nectarines, pitted and sliced (or substitute 4 cups canned or frozen slices)

⅓ cup honey

1. Preheat the oven to 375°F.
2. Mix together the almonds, sugar, granola, oats, melted butter, and almond extract in a medium-sized bowl.
3. Place the peaches in a 2-quart baking dish, drizzle the honey over the top, and toss to mix. Cover with the granola topping.
4. Bake on the middle shelf for 40 minutes, or until golden.

Plumcot-Lime Crisp

MAKES 8 SERVINGS

1 cup all-purpose flour

¾ cup firmly packed brown sugar

1 teaspoon poppy seeds

½ cup (1 stick) butter, sliced and chilled

3 pounds ripe plumcots or apricots, pitted and quartered (7–8 cups)

Juice of 2 limes (4 tablespoons)

Zest of 2 limes (4 teaspoons)

½ cup granulated sugar

1. Preheat the oven to 375°F.
2. Mix the flour, brown sugar, and poppy seeds in a medium-sized mixing bowl. Cut in the butter with a pastry blender or knife until the mixture forms large crumbs.
3. Mix the plumcots, lime juice, zest, and granulated sugar in a 9- by 11-inch baking dish. Spoon the flour mixture over the top.
4. Bake on the middle shelf for 30 to 40 minutes, or until golden.

Nectarine-Blueberry Crisp

MAKES 6-8 SERVINGS

⅓ cup firmly packed brown sugar

⅓ cup sifted all-purpose flour

⅓ cup rolled oats

1 teaspoon ground cinnamon

⅓ cup butter (5⅓ tablespoons), sliced and chilled

⅓ cup chopped pecans

2 pounds (5–6) nectarines, pitted, sliced, and cut into chunks

2 cups blueberries

½ cup granulated sugar

Nectarines and blueberries (and peaches) are at peak harvest in August, so take advantage and bake them together. They make beautiful crisps, cobblers, and pies, as well as many other delicious desserts.

1. Preheat the oven to 375°F.
2. Mix the brown sugar, flour, oats, and cinnamon in a large bowl. Cut in the butter with a pastry blender or knife until the mixture forms large crumbs. Stir in the pecans.
3. Combine the nectarines, blueberries, and granulated sugar in a 2-quart baking dish and spoon the flour mixture evenly over the top.
4. Bake in the middle of the oven for 40 minutes, or until golden.

READY-TO-GO CRISP TOPPING FOR INSTANT DESSERTS

When making your favorite crisp topping, double or triple the recipe and store the extra in plastic freezer bags. Label and freeze for up to 6 months. When the mood strikes or you're cooking for guests, tip canned or frozen sliced peaches, plums, or apricots into a baking dish, sprinkle with the frozen topping, and bake 45 to 50 minutes in a 350°F oven.

Peach Brown Betty

I had my first taste of Brown Betty about 25 years ago, not long after arriving in the United States. I loved it because it is very similar to English bread pudding. The traditional version is made with apple, but it is equally delicious when made with peaches, apricots, or plums. Serve with vanilla custard, yogurt, ice cream, or butterscotch pudding.

Butter-flavored cooking oil spray

6 large slices oatmeal or whole wheat bread

¾ cup brown sugar

1 teaspoon ground allspice

½ cup (1 stick) butter, melted

2 pounds (5–6) peaches or nectarines, pitted and sliced (or substitute 30 ounces canned slices, drained and juice reserved)

½ cup peach nectar (or reserved peach juice if using canned)

1. Preheat the oven to 350°F. Spray a 9- by 7-inch (2-quart) baking dish with butter-flavored cooking oil spray.
2. Crumble the bread into a large bowl, add the sugar and allspice, and stir in the butter.
3. Cover the bottom of the baking dish with one third of the crumb mixture. Spoon half the peach slices over the top and follow with another layer of crumbs, then peaches, and a final layer of crumbs. Pour the peach nectar over the top and cover the dish with aluminum foil.
4. Bake on the lower shelf of the oven for 30 minutes. Remove the foil and bake 20 to 30 minutes longer, or until the top is golden brown. Serve warm.

Mother's Plum and Raspberry Cobbler

1 pound plums, pitted and sliced (about 2 cups)

2 cups fresh or dry-pack frozen raspberries

⅓ cup sugar to make the fruit mixture, plus ¼ cup to make the dough

½ tablespoon water

1 cup all-purpose flour

½ teaspoon baking soda

½ teaspoon ground cinnamon

¼ cup sugar

4 tablespoons (½ stick) butter

2–4 tablespoons milk

At 95, my mother finds cobblers and crisps easier to whip together than pies. She makes at least one cobbler a week with fresh and frozen homegrown raspberries, gooseberries, black currants, blackberries, and rhubarb. She frequently uses two-fruit combinations, which, in season, often include apples or plums.

1. Preheat the oven to 375°F.
2. Combine the plums, raspberries, ⅓ cup of sugar, and the water in a saucepan. Cover and cook over low heat, stirring once or twice, for 10 minutes. Spoon into a 9- by 7-inch (2-quart) baking dish.
3. Sift the flour, baking soda, and cinnamon into a medium-sized bowl.
4. Stir the remaining ¼ cup of sugar into the flour mixture; cut in the butter with a pastry blender or knife. When the mixture is crumbly, stir in the milk to make a stiff, sconelike dough.
5. Spoon the dough over the top of the fruit mixture.
6. Bake in the middle of the oven for 25 to 30 minutes, or until the topping is golden-colored and a knife inserted in the center comes out clean.

Dried Plum and Pear Cobbler

MAKES 6-8 SERVINGS

Cobbler toppings usually resemble scone or biscuit dough. This one, however, is more like a cake. If you prefer, substitute one of the other toppings in this chapter.

1. Preheat the oven to 375°F. Spray a 2½-quart baking dish with butter-flavored cooking oil spray.
2. Mix the dried plums, pears, nectar, light brown sugar, ginger, and nutmeg in the baking dish.
3. Cream the butter and sugar together for 2 minutes with an electric blender in a medium-sized bowl. Beat in the eggs and vanilla.
4. Sift the flour and baking powder into the bowl and beat 1 to 2 minutes, or until blended.
5. Spoon the batter over the fruit and sprinkle the top with the 1 tablespoon of brown sugar.
6. Bake in the middle of the oven for 40 minutes, until golden brown and a knife or toothpick inserted in the center of the cake comes out clean.

Butter-flavored cooking oil spray

1 cup sliced dried plums

5 large pears (peeled if desired), cored and cut in ½-inch-thick slices

½ cup apricot nectar

½ cup firmly packed light brown sugar

½ teaspoon ground ginger

½ teaspoon ground nutmeg

¾ cup (1½ sticks) butter, softened

¾ cup granulated sugar

2 eggs

1 tablespoon vanilla extract

1½ cups all-purpose flour

2 teaspoons baking powder

1 tablespoon brown sugar

Peach-Pecan Kuchen

Butter-flavored cooking oil spray

1¼ cups all-purpose flour, plus 1 tablespoon

¼ cup granulated sugar

½ teaspoon baking powder

6 tablespoons butter, chilled

1 egg, beaten

3 tablespoons nonfat milk

Juice of ⅓ lemon
(1 tablespoon)

1½ pounds ripe peaches or nectarines, pitted and sliced (about 3 cups)

½ cup firmly packed brown sugar

1 teaspoon ground cinnamon

1 cup pecan halves

2 tablespoons honey

2 tablespoons butter, melted

This is like a single-crust pie, but easier to make because there's no need to roll the dough.

1. Preheat the oven to 400°F. Spray a 9-inch, loose-bottomed flan or pie pan with butter-flavored cooking oil spray.
2. Mix the flour, granulated sugar, and baking powder in a medium-sized bowl. Cut in the chilled butter with a pastry blender or knife until the mixture is crumbly. Add the egg, milk, and lemon juice and stir until the mixture forms a mass.
3. Place the dough in the center of the pan and press it across the bottom and up the sides.
4. Arrange the peach slices in concentric circles over the dough. Mix the brown sugar, the 1 tablespoon of flour, and the cinnamon and spoon evenly over the peaches. Arrange the pecan halves over the sugar mixture.
5. Stir the honey into the melted butter and drizzle over the top.
6. Place on the bottom shelf of the oven and bake for 15 minutes. Reduce the heat to 350°F and continue baking for 25 to 30 minutes longer. Cool on a wire rack and push the pan base free of the sides.

Eden Garden's Apricot Kugen

Mary Anne Brenkwitz (see the Brenkwitz Family profile, page 14) makes a crust with Bisquick's biscuit recipe. For ease of reference, I call for a shortcake crust here. Mary Anne says the sour cream topping can be reduced by half, but that it's especially delicious when made as directed.

1. Preheat the oven to 350°F.
2. Place the apricots, 1 cup of the sugar, and 1 teaspoon of the cinnamon in a large bowl and smash together with a potato masher.
3. Combine the flour, 2 tablespoons of the sugar, baking powder, and remaining ½ teaspoon of cinnamon in a medium-sized mixing bowl. Cut in the butter with a pastry blender or knife until the mixture forms large crumbs.
4. Mix the beaten egg and milk in a small bowl and pour into the crumb mixture. Stir until the dough clings together. Form into a ball with floured fingers and press into a 9- by 13-inch baking pan. Pour the apricot mixture into the pan.
5. Beat the sour cream, eggs, 1 cup sugar, cornstarch and salt for 1 to 2 minutes with an electric beater until smooth.
6. Pour the topping over the apricots.
7. Bake in the middle of the oven for 1 hour, or until the topping is golden and set.

4 pounds soft-ripe apricots, halved and pitted (about 10 cups)

2 cups sugar, plus 2 table-spoons

1½ teaspoons ground cinnamon

1 cup all-purpose flour

1 teaspoon baking powder

4 tablespoons butter

1 egg, beaten

¼ cup milk (or substitute rice or soy milk)

1 pint sour cream

6 eggs

¼ cup cornstarch

⅛ teaspoon salt

Cheesecake with Toasted Apricots

MAKES 12 SERVINGS

Butter-flavored cooking oil spray

¾ cup finely crushed graham crackers

2 tablespoons butter, melted

1 cup low-fat or nonfat cottage cheese

¼ cup nonfat milk

16 ounces nonfat cream cheese, cut up

¾ cup sugar, plus 3 tablespoons

2 tablespoons sifted all-purpose flour

Juice of 1 lemon (about 2 tablespoons)

1 tablespoon vanilla extract

¾ cup egg white substitute or 3 eggs, beaten

1 pound ripe apricots (about 8), halved and pitted

3 tablespoons butter

This really is a dream of a cheesecake. The luscious filling is quite low in fat.

1. Preheat the oven to 350°F. Spray a 9-inch springform pan with butter-flavored cooking oil spray.

2. Mix the cracker crumbs and melted butter in the springform pan and press over the bottom and a little way up the sides. Bake for 10 minutes, or until crisp. Remove to a wire rack to cool.

3. Place the cottage cheese and milk in a food processor and process until smooth. Add the cream cheese, the ¾ cup of sugar, flour, lemon juice, and vanilla and process until smooth. Add egg white substitute and pulse to mix. Pour the mixture into the cooled crust.

4. Place the pan on a baking sheet in the middle of the oven. Bake 40 minutes, until almost set in the center. To test for a good set, gently shake the pan. If the center jiggles, bake 5 minutes longer and test again. Remove to a wire rack and cool completely. Cover and refrigerate for at least 3 hours before releasing the springform sides.

5. To broil the apricots, place the apricot halves, cut-side up, on a baking sheet and add a knob of the butter to each cavity and sprinkle with the remaining sugar. Broil 4 inches from the heat for about 6 minutes, until the butter has melted and the sugar caramelized. Remove from the heat and cool. Slice the apricots into quarters and arrange on top of the chilled cheesecake.

Dried Fruit Compotes in Liqueur

Some of the best dried fruit compotes I've ever tasted have been on breakfast buffet tables in Turkey, Spain, and South Africa. The two below are definitely intended for the dessert table. Make 1-pint jars to give away as holiday or hostess gifts.

1. Scald two 1-pint jars.
2. Mix the water and sugar in a saucepan. Bring to a boil over high heat, stirring until the sugar is dissolved. Remove the syrup from the heat and add the cinnamon stick.
3. In the first jar, alternate ½-cup layers of peaches and apricots. Discard the cinnamon stick from the syrup. Pour the peach brandy and 2 cups of the syrup over the dried fruits. Run a knife between the fruit and the jar to eliminate air bubbles. Close the jar with a tight clamp or screw-top lid. Place in a cool, dark cupboard for at least 2 weeks.
4. In the second jar, repeat the process with the plums, cherries, plum brandy, and remaining 2 cups of syrup.

4 cups water

2 cups sugar

1 cinnamon stick

2 cups dried peaches

2 cups dried apricots

½ cup peach or apricot brandy

2 cups pitted dried plums

2 cups dried cherries

½ cup plum or cherry brandy

Eden Garden's Apricot Pie

MAKES 8 SERVINGS

3 pounds apricots, pitted and chopped (about 5 cups)

1 teaspoon lemon juice

1 cup sugar

¼ cup all-purpose flour

¼ teaspoon ground cinnamon

Pastry for a 9-inch double-crust pie (see page 166) or 2 store-bought refrigerator piecrusts (9 inches each)

2 tablespoons butter, diced

Mary Anne Brenkwitz makes a delicious pie that can be thrown together with refrigerator piecrusts and baked in a jiffy.

1. Preheat the oven to 425°F.
2. Place the apricots and lemon juice in a medium-sized bowl. Mix in the sugar, flour, and cinnamon.
3. Spoon the mixture into the prepared pie shell and dot with the butter. Cover with the prepared top crust, make three steam vents in the center, trim, seal, and flute.
4. Cover the edges of the crust with 2- to 3-inch strips of aluminum foil to prevent excessive browning. Bake in the middle of the oven for 35 to 45 minutes, or until the crust is golden brown and juice begins to bubble through the steam vents. Remove the foil during last 15 minutes of baking.

FREEZING BAKED PIES

Cool until completely cold before enclosing baked pies in freezer bags. A warm pie will create condensation in the freezer bag, resulting in a moist and soggy crust. To bake a frozen baked pie, move it directly from the freezer into a preheated 375°F oven for approximately 30 minutes. Cover the top with aluminum foil if the crust starts to get too brown.

Bishop's Chèvre Cheesecake with Apricot Brandy Syrup

John Bishop serves this unusual cheesecake with dried apricots in apricot brandy. If you don't have apricot brandy at hand, you can substitute regular brandy, Grand Marnier, or another fruit liqueur.

1. Slice the apricots and peaches to the same size as the cherries.
2. Combine the water, ½ cup of the sugar, and the brandy in a saucepan. Bring to a boil over medium heat and add the dried fruit and the cinnamon stick.
3. Cut the vanilla bean in half lengthwise, scrape out the seeds, and add, with the husk, to the boiling fruit. Reduce the heat to low and simmer, uncovered, for 10 minutes.
4. Remove from the heat, cover, and steep for 30 minutes. Remove and discard the vanilla husk and cinnamon stick.
5. Cool and refrigerate in a covered container. (The compote will keep in the refrigerator for up to 3 weeks.)
6. Preheat the oven to 300°F.

(continued on facing page)

1 cup mix of dried apricots, peaches, and cherries

1 cup water

1½ cups sugar

¼ cup apricot brandy

1 cinnamon stick

1 vanilla bean

2 packages (8 ounces each) cream cheese

12 ounces soft goat cheese

5 eggs

Juice of 1 lemon (3 tablespoons)

Zest of 1 lemon (1 tablespoon)

3 tablespoons all-purpose flour

7. Cream together the remaining 1 cup of sugar, the cream cheese, and the goat cheese in an electric mixer. Beat in the eggs, one at a time, and then the lemon juice, zest, and flour.

8. Pour the batter into a 9-inch springform pan. Wrap a piece of aluminum foil around the bottom of the pan to prevent water from leaking through the cracks during baking. Place the springform pan in a roasting pan and pour boiling water in the pan, halfway up the sides of the springform pan.

9. Bake until the cake just wiggles in the center when the pan is tapped on the side, about 1 hour.

10. Remove from the oven and allow the cake to cool in the pan of water. When the water has cooled to room temperature, lift out the springform pan and remove the foil. Cover and refrigerate for at least 2 hours before removing the sides of the springform pan.

11. To serve, use a hot knife to cut wedges of cheesecake. Place on plates and spoon the fruit and syrup over the top.

POACHING

Cut the fruits in half and remove the pits; leave in halves or slice. Place in a pan with just enough juice, wine, or water to cover. Add a pinch of ground nutmeg and ginger, a handful of cinnamon basil leaves, lemon balm leaves, lime or orange zest, or any other flavor that will complement the dish they will be accompanying. Place over medium-high heat. When bubbles form around the edges, reduce the heat to low and simmer 15 minutes, or until tender.

Single-Crust Rustic Pie

MAKES 8 SERVINGS OR ONE 10-INCH PIE

Rolling out one large crust to pull up around a fruit filling instead of messing about with two crusts is an easy way to make a pie. An open rustic pie is also more appealing to those who prefer tarts over two-crust pies (yours truly included). You can use any or a mix of the fruits called for to make a rustic pie. Adjust the spices and sugar to flavor and sweeten tarter plums or apricots, or reduce the amount of sugar for very sweet peaches and nectarines. Bake this on a pie plate or free-form on a pizza pan or baking sheet.

Butter-flavored cooking oil spray

2 cups all-purpose flour, plus 2 tablespoons

10 tablespoons (1 stick plus 2 tablespoons) butter, diced and chilled

4–5 tablespoons ice-cold water

2 pounds ripe apricots, peaches, nectarines, or plums, pitted and cut into ½-inch slices (about 4 cups)

⅓–½ cup light brown sugar

1 tablespoon melted butter (optional)

½–1 teaspoon mix of ground spices, including cinnamon, ginger, and nutmeg

1. Preheat the oven to 425°F. Spray a 10-inch pie plate or a pizza pan with butter-flavored cooking oil spray.

2. Place the 2 cups of flour into the bowl of a food processor or large mixing bowl. Add the butter and pulse, or cut in the butter by hand with a pastry blender or knife, until the mixture forms large crumbs.

3. Sprinkle 3 tablespoons of the ice water over the mixture and pulse again or stir together with a fork. Add more water, 1 tablespoon at a time, until the dough is moistened and forms a mass.

4. Remove the dough to a board lightly dusted with flour or finely crushed cookie crumbs and roll it into a 14-inch circle. Fold in half and slide into the prepared pan. Unfold, leaving a 3- to 4-inch overhang.

(continued on facing page)

5. Arrange the fruit in the center of the dough.
6. Mix the light brown sugar with the 2 tablespoons of flour and the ground spices and sprinkle the fruit with the mixture.
7. Bring up the overhanging dough around the fruit toward the center, folding it to fit neatly. Place the pie plate on a baking tray on the middle shelf of the oven. Bake 15 minutes.
8. Reduce the temperature to 375°F. Brush with the melted butter (if using) and bake for 30 minutes longer, until the filling is bubbling and the crust is golden. Cover loosely with foil during the last 10 to 15 minutes if the crust begins to darken too quickly.
9. Remove to a wire rack to cool.

NOTE: The pastry in this recipe is also sufficient to make a two-crust pie or a top crust for a large deep-dish pie.

FREEZING EXTRA FILLING FOR A TART

Place the remaining filling in a gallon-sized freezer bag. Squeeze out as much air as possible and seal the bag tightly. Place in a 9-inch pie plate and press the filling to fit. Freeze the shaped filling in the pie plate, removing the plate after the filling has frozen. When ready to bake, remove the filling from the freezer bag into an unbaked frozen pie shell. Bake in a preheated 425°F oven for 30 minutes, then reduce the heat to 375°F and bake 30 minutes longer. If desired, make a crisp or crumb topping and sprinkle over the filling 30 minutes before the end of baking. Thaw the filling when using with fresh-made or thawed pie pastry.

Cookie-Cutter Crust Deep-Dish Plum Pie

*M*ake this with sweet prune plums or use large ripe plums. Otherwise, substitute canned plums or apricots.

1. Preheat the oven to 375°F.
2. Cook the plums and lemon juice in a medium-size saucepan over medium heat for 10 minutes, to soften. Spoon into a 9-inch square baking dish.
3. Mix the sugar, ginger, nutmeg, and tapioca and sprinkle the mixture over the plums. Dot with the butter if using.
4. Roll the unbaked tart crust into a 12-inch square and cut it into cookie-cutter shapes, squares, circles, or lattice strips. Fit the shapes or lattice neatly over the fruit.
5. Bake for 45 minutes, until the crust is golden brown and the filling is bubbling.

2 pounds plums, halved and pitted

Juice of ⅓ lemon (1 tablespoon)

¾–1 cup sugar, depending on acidity of fruit

¼ teaspoon ground ginger

¼ teaspoon ground nutmeg

2 tablespoons quick-cooking tapioca

1 tablespoon butter, diced (optional)

1 unbaked crust for a 9- or 10-inch tart (see page 164; do not roll the dough into a circle or place in a pie pan)

FREEZING UNBAKED PIES

Assemble the pastry and filling as usual without cutting steam vents in the top crust. Freeze in the pie plate. When frozen solid, slip the pie out of the pie plate and place in a large freezer bag. To bake a frozen unbaked pie, cut three or four steam vents in the top crust and bake immediately in a preheated 425°F oven for 30 minutes. Reduce the heat to 375°F and bake for 30 to 40 minutes longer. Cover the crust with aluminum foil if it starts to get too brown.

Nectarine-Plum Clafouti

Butter-flavored cooking oil spray

3 eggs or ¾ cup egg substitute

1½ cups milk

½ cup sugar

½ teaspoon ground cinnamon

½ teaspoon ground nutmeg

¾ cup all-purpose flour

1 pound nectarines, pitted and sliced (2 cups)

1 pound plums, pitted and sliced (2 cups)

1 tablespoon confectioners' sugar

Clafouti is a classic French dessert usually associated with cherries. However, this melt-in-the-mouth egg custard batter is just as delicious when combined with the larger stone fruits. Substitute fresh prune plums, pluots, apricots, or peaches — they all produce winning flavors.

1. Preheat the oven to 375°F. Spray a 10-inch oval gratin dish or a 9- by 7-inch baking dish with butter-flavored cooking oil spray.
2. Beat together the eggs, milk, sugar, cinnamon, and nutmeg in a large bowl. Stir in the flour and beat until mixed.
3. Place the fruit in the baking dish and pour the batter over the top. Bake in the middle of the oven for 35 to 40 minutes, until the batter has set and the top is golden. Cool on a wire rack for 20 minutes.
4. Sprinkle with the confectioners' sugar and serve warm.

Fresh White Peach Tart

MAKES FILLING FOR A 9- OR 10-INCH TART

This is a fabulously easy tart to whip up. If desired, sprinkle with a few fresh raspberries.

1 block (8 ounces) nonfat cream cheese, sliced

½ cup raspberries

¼ cup sugar

1 baked crust for a 9- or 10-inch tart (see page 164)

4 large white peaches or nectarines (peeled if desired), pitted and sliced (3 cups)

½ cup seedless raspberry jam

1. Mix the cream cheese, raspberries, and sugar in a medium-sized bowl and beat with an electric mixer for 2 minutes, until smooth. Spread over the baked tart shell and arrange the peach slices decoratively over the top.
2. Melt the raspberry jam in a small saucepan over low heat. Spoon over the peaches. Refrigerate at least 2 hours before serving.

Traditional Peach Pie

MAKES FILLING FOR ONE 9-INCH PIE

2 tablespoons peach or apricot jam, at room temperature

Pastry for a 9-inch double-crust pie (see page 166)

3 pounds peaches, sliced (6 cups)

¾ cup plus 2 tablespoons sugar

¼ cup cornstarch

½ teaspoon ground cinnamon

1. Preheat the oven to 425°F.
2. Spread the jam evenly over the pastry shell; refrigerate.
3. Mix the peaches with the ¾ cup of sugar and the cornstarch in a large bowl. (If the peaches are very juicy, refer to page 166, Step 6.)
4. Spoon the peaches into the chilled pie shell and cover with the top crust. Trim, flute, and bake according to the directions on page 166.

Plumcot–Dried Plum Phyllo Turnovers

Butter-flavored cooking oil spray

1 pound plumcots or apricots, pitted and diced (about 2 cups)

¼ cup snipped dried plums

¼ cup sugar

1 tablespoon all-purpose flour

½ teaspoon ground ginger

6 sheets phyllo pastry

Thank goodness for phyllo pastry and the fact that we can buy it ready-made. Sometimes it seems like the ultimate convenience ingredient because it's so meltingly crispy and crunchy, and so light and low in fat. Make these delectable turnovers with plums or peaches and blueberries, dried apricots, or cherries. Serve with sorbet, sherbet, or ice cream.

1. Preheat the oven to 375°F. Spray a baking sheet with butter-flavored cooking oil spray.

2. Mix the plumcots, dried plums, sugar, flour, and ginger in a medium-sized bowl.

3. Follow the package instructions for handling the phyllo pastry. Keep it damp while preparing the turnovers.

4. Lightly spray the oil on one sheet of phyllo pastry. Place another sheet of phyllo pastry on top of the first sheet and spray it as well. Top with the third sheet, but do not spray the top. Cut the three sheets lengthwise in four pieces.

5. Lay the pieces vertically on the counter and spoon ¼ cup of the plumcot filling about 2 inches from the end closest to you. Fold the end over the filling at a 45-degree angle. Continue folding the entire length to form a triangular shape.

6. Repeat steps 4 and 5 with the remaining three strips of phyllo and filling. Place the turnovers on the prepared baking sheet.

7. Bake 20 minutes, or until golden and flaky. Serve warm.

Fruit Shortcake

Shortcakes are scones in disguise. Choose any of the stone fruits to top the shortcake; they all taste equally good. While we tend to associate shortcakes with summer fruits, canned or frozen fruits are more than satisfactory options in winter.

1. Preheat the oven to 350°F. Spray a 9-inch pie plate with butter-flavored cooking oil spray.
2. Mix the flour, sugar, baking powder, and cinnamon in a medium-sized mixing bowl. Cut in the butter with a pastry blender or knife until the mixture forms large crumbs.
3. Combine the egg white substitute and milk in a small bowl and pour into the crumb mixture. Stir until the dough clings together. Form into a ball with floured fingers and press into the pie plate.
4. Bake in the middle of the oven for 20 to 25 minutes, or until golden. Place the pie dish on a wire rack and cool for 5 minutes.
5. Arrange the sliced peaches over the shortcake and spoon the yogurt or frosting over the top. Serve immediately.

Butter-flavored cooking oil spray

1 cup all-purpose flour

2 tablespoons sugar

1 teaspoon baking powder

½ teaspoon ground cinnamon

¼ cup butter

¼ cup egg substitute or 1 egg, beaten

¼ cup low-fat or nonfat milk (or substitute rice milk or soy milk)

1 pound peaches, nectarines, plums, or apricots, pitted and sliced (2 cups) (or substitute 16 ounces canned peaches or apricots, drained)

1 cup creamy nonfat vanilla yogurt

Fruit Pie with Baked Nut Streusel Crust

MAKES 8 SERVINGS

1 cup all-purpose flour

½ cup sliced almonds or chopped pecans

⅓ cup confectioners' sugar

6 tablespoons butter, sliced and chilled

1 egg, beaten

1 tablespoon ice-cold water

3–4 cups sliced peaches, nectarines, or plums (or substitute canned slices, drained)

½ cup melted peach or apricot jam

After baking 10 minutes, this crust can be filled with fruits and returned to the oven for 30 to 35 minutes, until the filling has cooked. If desired, reserve some of the crumbly nut streusel to sprinkle over the filling before baking.

1. Preheat the oven to 400°F.
2. Put the flour, almonds, and sugar in a food processor and pulse to mix. Add the butter and pulse until the mixture is crumbly. Add the egg and cold water and pulse just until the dough forms a mass.
3. Remove the dough and press into a 9- or 10-inch pie plate or 9-inch square baking dish. Prick all over the bottom with a fork. Refrigerate 1 hour or longer.
4. Bake on the bottom shelf of the oven for 10 minutes. Prick the shell again and bake 15 minutes longer, or until golden brown.
5. Fill with the fruit slices.
6. Glaze with the jam.

MEASURING BY WEIGHT

Most varieties of peaches and nectarines don't vary much in size. Of course, there are some super-large peaches that are the equivalent of two medium-sized peaches and large peaches tend to be larger than large nectarines. On the whole, however, most varieties of peaches and nectarines don't vary tremendously in size. But varieties of apricots and, particularly, plums do vary tremendously in size. For this reason, measuring by weight or in cups will give you the most accurate results.

Eden Garden's Tart

MAKES ONE 9- OR 10-INCH TART

½ cup almond paste, crumbled

¼ cup butter

2 eggs

2 tablespoons all-purpose flour

2 tablespoons sugar

1 unbaked crust for a 9- or 10-inch tart
(see page 164)

2 apricots, pitted and sliced

2 pluots, pitted and sliced

2 tablespoons sliced almonds

¼ cup apricot preserves, melted

1. Preheat the oven to 400°F.
2. Place the almond paste, butter, eggs, flour, and sugar in a food processor and pulse until smooth. Pour into the tart shell.
3. Arrange the apricots and pluots over the filling and sprinkle with the almonds.
4. Bake for 35 minutes, or until golden brown. Cool completely before removing the sides of the pan.
5. To serve, brush the top with the melted apricot preserves.

Walnut Prune Tart

FILLING FOR A 9- OR 10-INCH TART

⅓ cup firmly packed brown sugar

⅓ cup honey

½ cup apple juice or water

1¼ cups chopped black
walnuts

1 cup snipped dried plums

1 unbaked crust for a 9- or 10-inch tart
(see page 164)

1. Preheat the oven to 375°F.
2. Bring the sugar, honey, and apple juice to a boil in a medium-sized saucepan over high heat, stirring until the sugar is dissolved. Reduce the heat to low and simmer, stirring occasionally, for 15 minutes.
3. Stir in the walnuts and dried plums. Return to a boil, reduce the heat to low, and simmer 10 minutes, stirring occasionally.
4. Spoon the filling into the prepared pie shell.
5. Bake in the middle of the oven for 35 to 45 minutes. Cool in the pan on a wire rack. Remove the pan sides before serving.

Kate Zurschmeide's Peach Pie with Cream Cheese Pastry

MAKES A DOUBLE-CRUST PIE OR TWO 9- OR 10-INCH SINGLE-CRUST PIES

FOR THE PASTRY

2½ cups all-purpose flour

10 tablespoons butter (1 stick plus 2 tablespoons), chilled and sliced

1 tablespoon sugar

¼ teaspoon baking powder

¼ teaspoon salt

½ cup low-fat cream cheese, cut into 1-inch cubes and chilled

2 tablespoons ice water

1 tablespoon apple cider vinegar

FOR THE FILLING

⅔ cup sugar

1 egg

⅓ cup melted butter

1 tablespoon cornstarch

1 tablespoon all-purpose flour

1 cup fresh raspberries

4 cups fresh peaches, peeled and sliced

TO MAKE THE PASTRY

1. Place the flour, butter, sugar, baking powder, and salt in a large bowl and mix together with a pastry blender or knife until lumpy. Cut in the cream cheese.
3. Mix the ice water and vinegar and stir into the flour mixture until the dough forms a mass.
4. Divide into two portions, one larger than the other, and flatten into circles. Place into plastic bags and refrigerate for 1 hour. See directions for Double Crust Pie, from Step 5, on page 166.

TO MAKE THE FILLING

1. Preheat the oven to 400°F.
2. Blend together the sugar, egg, melted butter, cornstarch, and flour in a small food processor or blender. Add ⅛ cup of the red raspberries and blend again until smooth.
3. Place the peaches and remaining raspberries in a large bowl and toss gently.
4. Spoon the peaches and raspberries into the prepared pie shell and pour the egg mixture on top. Cover with the pastry strips arranged in lattice fashion. Trim and flute.
5. Bake in the middle of the oven for 50 minutes, or until golden.

Eiffel Tower's Tarte Tatin

MAKES 8–10 SERVINGS

Madelaine Sosnitsky, owner of the Eiffel Tower in my hometown of Leesburg, Virginia, says that chef Patrick Masrevery makes "the best Tarte Tatin I ever had." Chef Masrevery makes the classic apple version, but you can use nectarines, peaches, apricots, or plums.

½ cup (1 stick) sweet butter

1 cup sugar (white or brown)

3 pounds firm-ripe nectarines or peaches, pitted and quartered

1 sheet puff pastry rolled into a 12-inch circle (or substitute unbaked crust for a 9-inch tart, but don't press the dough into the pan; leave as a 12-inch circle (see page 164)

1. Preheat the oven to 400°F. Soften the butter in a 12- to 13-inch, deep-sided, heavy ovenproof skillet over low heat. Spread the sugar evenly over the butter and arrange the nectarine quarters in concentric rings over the top. Arrange as many quarters as it takes to make a tight fit, until you can no longer see the sugar.

2. Raise the heat to medium and cook the nectarine quarters about 10 minutes, until the sugar caramelizes and starts to bubble under and around them.

3. Remove the pan from the heat and cover the nectarines with the pastry. Place the skillet in the oven and bake for 20 minutes, or until the crust is golden.

4. Remove the skillet from the oven and set it on a wire rack. Cool the tart in the skillet for 2 to 3 hours.

5. Before serving, place the skillet over low heat on the stovetop for about 5 minutes, until the caramel melts and you can slide the tart around. Remove from the skillet by turning it upside down onto a large plate.

6. Serve immediately

Apricot Pudding

Butter-flavored cooking oil spray

3 tablespoons apricot jam

1 cup snipped dried apricots

4 large slices nutty whole wheat bread, processed or rubbed into coarse crumbs

½ cup firmly packed brown sugar

½ cup sifted all-purpose flour

½ teaspoon baking powder

½ teaspoon baking soda

1 teaspoon ground allspice

1 teaspoon ground cinnamon

1 teaspoon ground ginger

4 tablespoons butter

½ cup nonfat milk (or substitute low-fat rice milk or soy milk)

½ cup egg substitute or 2 eggs, beaten

The British are famous for their bread and sponge puddings made with fresh or dried fruits, marmalade, syrup, or jam preserves. I grew up eating at least one kind of pudding a week because they were as common a "sweet" as the pies, crumbles, and cakes my mother made daily. It is no wonder that pudding is the common term for "sweet" or "dessert" in England. Serve with vanilla yogurt or vanilla pudding.

1. Preheat the oven to 350°F. Spray a 2-quart baking dish with butter-flavored cooking oil spray.
2. Spread the jam over the bottom of the baking dish.
3. Mix the apricots, bread crumbs, brown sugar, flour, baking powder, baking soda, allspice, cinnamon, and ginger in a large bowl.
4. Melt the butter in a small saucepan over low heat. Remove from the heat; stir in the milk and egg substitute. Stir into the bread mixture and spoon into the prepared baking dish.
5. Bake in the middle of the oven for 50 minutes. Serve warm.

Tart Crust

This simple recipe for a tart crust can be knocked together and rolled out in just a few minutes.

FOR AN UNBAKED CRUST:

1. Place the flour into the bowl of a food processor or large mixing bowl. Pulse or cut in the butter by hand with a pastry blender or knife until the mixture forms large crumbs. Sprinkle the ice water over the mixture and pulse or stir together with a fork until the dough is moistened and forms a mass. If necessary, add more water, 1 teaspoon at a time. Remove the dough from the bowl and shape into a ball.

2. On a lightly floured surface, flatten the dough and roll it into a 12-inch circle. Ease the pastry into a 9- or 10-inch pie plate or tart pan with a removable bottom, sprayed with cooking oil. Press the pastry over the bottom and up the sides of the plate or pan. Chill in the refrigerator for 15 to 30 minutes or in the freezer for 5 minutes. If baking the crust without a filling, refrigerate for 1 hour or freeze for 15 minutes.

FOR A BAKED CRUST:

3. Preheat the oven to 450°F. Prick the bottom of the pastry all over with the tines of a fork. Bake in the middle of the oven for 12 to 15 minutes, or until crisp and golden. Cool on a wire rack.

1 cup all-purpose flour

4 tablespoons butter (½ stick)

3 tablespoons ice-cold water

MAKE-AHEAD PASTRY

This gets you one step ahead of the game. Make the pastry, divide it into two equal pieces, and roll them into 9-inch rounds. Wrap individually in wax paper and place in gallon-sized freezer bags. Place on a firm base (a pizza pan or plate works well) and refrigerate for up to 3 days or freeze and thaw in the refrigerator or at room temperature before using.

Pressed-Nut Cookie Crust

An easy shortbread cookie crust delicious with any fresh fruit filling or try Bishop's Poached Peaches (see page 133).

Butter-flavored cooking oil spray

1½ cups all-purpose flour

1 cup firmly packed brown sugar

½ cup chopped walnuts

1 teaspoon ground cinnamon

½ cup butter (1 stick), sliced and chilled

1. Preheat the oven to 425°F. Spray a 9-inch pie dish with butter-flavored cooking oil spray.
2. Pulse the flour, sugar, walnuts, and cinnamon in a food processor to mix. Add the butter and pulse until the mixture is crumbly. Press 2 cups of the mixture onto the bottom and up the sides of the pie dish.
3. Bake on the lower shelf for 5 minutes. Remove and spoon fruit filling into the crust. Sprinkle remaining walnut mixture over the top and bake 40 minutes.

No-Bake Crumb Crust

Fill this delicious cereal crust with fresh sliced fruits or Peaches in Caramel Sauce (see page 132).

⅓ cup butter

⅓ cup firmly packed light brown sugar

2 cups cereal flakes, crushed (about 1½ cups crumbs)

1. Melt the butter with the sugar in a small saucepan until the mixture boils; remove from the heat. Stir in the cereal crumbs.
2. Press the mixture over the bottom and sides of a 9- or 10-inch pie dish, a 9-inch square baking dish, or a 9-inch springform pan.
3. Refrigerate for at least 30 minutes before filling.

Pastry for a Double-Crust Pie

PASTRY FOR A 9-INCH DOUBLE-CRUST PIE

This recipe provides sufficient pastry for two 9-inch pie crusts or 6 to 8 turnovers or dumplings. The lemon juice helps to relax the rich dough, making it easier to roll out.

1. Preheat the oven to 425°F. Spray a 9-inch pie plate with butter-flavored cooking oil spray.
2. Place the flour in the bowl of a food processor or large mixing bowl. Add butter, and sugar (if using) and pulse, or cut in the butter with a pastry blender or knife until the mixture resembles large crumbs.
3. Sprinkle 3 tablespoons of the ice water over the mixture and pulse or stir together with a fork. Add the lemon juice and more water, 1 tablespoon at a time, until the dough is moistened enough to form a mass.
4. Divide the dough into two pieces and flatten into 6-inch disks. Wrap in plastic wrap or drop into plastic bags and refrigerate for 30 to 60 minutes.
5. Roll out one disk into a 12-inch circle about ⅛ inch thick. Loosely fold the circle in half and drop the crease onto the center of the greased pie plate. Gently press the pastry over the bottom and up the sides. Trim around the edge, leaving a ½- to 1-inch overhang.
6. Brush the crust with the beaten egg white (this will help prevent the bottom from becoming soggy when using juicy fruit fillings). Refrigerate for about 30 minutes while making the pie filling of choice, or freeze while rolling out the second crust.

(continued on facing page)

Butter-flavored cooking oil spray

2½ cups sifted all-purpose flour

12 tablespoons butter, sliced and chilled

2 tablespoons sugar (eliminate for savory dishes)

6 tablespoons ice-cold water

Juice of about 1 lemon (1 tablespoon) (or substitute vinegar)

1 egg white, beaten (or substitute 2 tablespoons melted apricot jam)

1 to 2 teaspoons sugar, optional

7. Roll out the second disk of dough into a 12-inch circle. Fold in half and place over the prepared filling, then unfold to fit. Trim excessive overhang as necessary. Press the edges together to seal and flute or crimp with the tines of a fork. Cut four steam vents in the center and sprinkle with 1 to 2 teaspoons of sugar, if desired.

8. Bake on the middle shelf of the oven for 15 minutes. Reduce the oven to 400°F and bake 40 minutes longer. If the edges of the crust start to brown too quickly, cover with strips of aluminum foil or a pie-saver shield. Cool completely before cutting.

PICK-A-FRUIT PIE

For the best-flavored pies, tarts, crisps, cobblers, and other deep-dish dessert recipes, use fully ripe fruit. When the fruit is ripe, you will also find you need to use less sugar.

To prepare sliced peaches, nectarines, plums, pluots, plumcots, and apricots, first wash and dry them. Cut in half, remove the pit (if necessary), and slice ½ inch thick.

Estimated quantities of fruit, sugar, and thickening agent are as follows:

Single-Crust Pie (deep-dish or tart): Use 2 to 2½ pounds (about 4 cups sliced) of fruit. Sweeten with ½ to ¾ cup of sugar, depending on how sweet or tart the fruit is. Thicken with 3 tablespoons of cornstarch. Mix the sugar and cornstarch and toss with the sliced fruit.

Double-Crust Pie: Use 3 to 3½ pounds (6 cups sliced) of fruit. Sweeten with ¾ to 1 cup of sugar, depending on how sweet or tart the fruit is. Thicken with ¼ cup of cornstarch. Mix the sugar and cornstarch and toss with the sliced fruit.

Cornmeal Crust

PASTRY FOR A 9- OR 10-INCH TART OR THIN LATTICE-TOPPED PIE

This makes a single-crust tart or a thin lattice-topped pie.

1. Preheat the oven to 375°F. Spray a 9- or 10-inch pie plate with butter-flavored cooking oil spray.

2. Put the flour and the cornmeal in a large mixing bowl. Cut in the butter by hand with a pastry blender or knife until the mixture resembles large crumbs. Stir in the sugar.

3. Sprinkle 3 tablespoons of the cold milk over the mixture and stir with a fork until the dough is moistened and forms a mass. If necessary, add the remaining tablespoon of milk.

4. Roll the dough into a 12-inch circle about ⅛ inch thick. (If you want enough dough to make a lattice-covered pie, roll into two 6-inch disks instead and follow the instructions for double-crust pie pastry on page 166.) Loosely fold the circle in half and drop the crease onto the center of the greased pie plate. Gently press the pastry over the bottom and up the sides. Trim around the edge and flute or crimp with the tines of a fork.

Butter-flavored cooking oil spray

1¼ cups all-purpose flour

¼ cup white cornmeal

½ cup (1 stick) butter, sliced and chilled

2 tablespoons sugar

4 tablespoons ice-cold, nonfat milk

HOW TO MAKE A LATTICE CRUST

Roll out one of the 6-inch disks of pastry into a 10- to 12-inch circle and use a fluted pastry wheel or sharp knife to cut it into ½- to ¾-inch-wide strips.

Reserving the longest for the center, arrange the strips ½ inch apart over the filling. Make a second layer across the top in the opposite direction to form a lattice design.

When all the strips are in place, press firmly around the edges to seal the crusts. Trim off any overhang and flute the crust or crimp with the tines of a fork.

Appendix:
Meet the Varieties

Orange and red may not be considered good colors when associated with weather forecasts, but as far as fruit is concerned, these bright colors spell good nutrition. Intensely pigmented fruits, such as peaches, nectarines, apricots, and plums, are powerful cocktails packed with antioxidant phytonutrients that fight disease.

A recent report from the United States Department of Agriculture states that per capita consumption of fresh fruit has increased during the last 30 years. Though this is largely the result of the ever-growing range of produce available in the supermarkets (a 94 percent increase since 1987), it can also be attributed to a heightened awareness of the health benefits of eating fruits and vegetables, which include reduced risk of cancer and coronary and age-related diseases.

In 1991 the National Cancer Institute and the USDA's Produce for Better Health Foundation formed the 5 A Day for Better Health program. They, along with other health organizations, recommended we consume a minimum of five servings of fruits and vegetables per day.

According to the NCI, the American Heart Association, and the American Diabetes Association, health studies have proved that eating seven to nine servings of fruits and vegetables each day provides us with the antioxidants we need for protection against heart disease, hyper-tension, diabetes, age-related eye diseases, pulmonary diseases, and cancers of the colon, pancreas, stomach, throat, larynx, lungs, and skin. Researchers have established the fact that these diseases are caused mainly by destructive molecules, known as free radicals, that attack and damage the body's immune system. Antioxidants help to neutralize free radicals and protect our bodies from further cell destruction.

It really is quite easy to eat five servings a day, especially when we include delectable summer fruits like peaches, nectarines, apricots, and plums in our diets. Plump, aromatic, and bursting with flavor when picked at perfection, they are a sweet and juicy source of nutrition because they are high in fiber, pectin, magnesium, potassium, beta-carotene/vitamin A, vitamin C, niacin, and riboflavin. If five servings sound like a lot, consider this: Three apricots (or one very large plum or one medium-large peach or nectarine) are considered the equivalent of one serving, which is a half-cup of cooked fruits or vegetables.

Fresh domestic peaches, nectarines, apricots, and plums are available from May to October. We can also eat these fruits canned, frozen, and dried year-round and still gain nutritional benefits because those grown for commercial processing are harvested and processed when they are in peak, tree-ripened condition. Research conducted at the University of Massachusetts found that recipes using canned fruits compared in taste and nutritional value to those made with fresh or frozen.

Dried fruits, particularly apricots and plums, are nutritional powerhouses because they are harvested when they have developed maximum sugar content. Ripe fruits contain higher concentrations of nutrients, which become even more concentrated when they are dried. Dried plums, in fact, are the leading antioxidant fruit. Though dried plums and apricots are known for their natural laxative effect, all four fruits aid our digestive processes, especially when we consume the skin. Removing the skin robs them of fiber, which plays a role in controlling high blood sugar and lowering blood cholesterol levels.

These four super fruits and their kin — apriums, pluots, and plumcots — are rich in phytonutrients (phytochemicals), natural chemical compounds produced by plants in addition to minerals and vitamins. Phytonutrients give plants color and flavor and provide antioxidants, which are known to help the body and immune system fight diseases. Our bodies naturally produce antioxidants, but as we get older, they produce less. Eating brightly pigmented fruits and vegetables helps to replenish our antioxidant levels.

The better-known phytonutrient groups are the carotenoids and flavonoids. Carotenoids are found mostly in yellow, orange, red, and green fruits and vegetables. Though there are hundreds of carotenoids, the more researched ones include the antioxidants beta-cryptoxanthin, lutein, zeaxanthin, lycopene, and beta-carotene, which the body converts to vitamin A. While peaches, nectarines, and apricots fall into the carotenoid group, they are also endowed with vitamin C, another powerful antioxidant.

Flavonoids are another large group of protective phytonutrients. Some of the most potent flavonoids are the antioxidants quercetin, anthocyanidin, luteolin, catechin, allicin, rutin, and hesperidin. High concentrations of flavonoids are found in blue, purple, red, and green fruits and vegetables and, of course, that group includes most plums, as well as red-orange nectarines and peaches. Flavonoids are also present in white fruits and vegetables including onions, garlic, and white nectarines and peaches, but not, alas, white potatoes.

These antioxidant compounds are much higher in tree-ripened fruits than in those that are immature and green. They also start to break down in overripe and bruised produce. This gives us two more reasons to try and find perfectly ripe fruits and know that those with firm, barely soft flesh and fragrant aromas promise sweet, flavorful eating with maximum nutrients.

A Buyer's Guide

While the following varieties are available in the United States, many are also grown throughout the rest of the world. You will find some of them in supermarkets, where they are rarely identified by variety, and even more varieties at local farmers' markets, farm stands, and orchards.

PEACHES

Variety	Description
MAY	
MAY CREST	Yellow with bright red blush and juicy, slightly tart, exceptionally peachy-flavored bright yellow flesh.
SPRINGCREST	Similar to May Crest; yellow with bright red blush and juicy, slightly tart, bright yellow flesh.
JUNE	
BELLE OF GEORGIA	Pink skinned with aromatic, sweet, juicy white flesh.
CRIMSON LADY	The almost smooth skin is bright yellow blushed with bright red-purple. The bright yellow flesh develops sweetness as the fruits ripen off the tree.
FLAVORCREST	Yellow lightly mottled with red-orange. The deep yellow flesh has the perfect balance of a high-acid, sweet-tart flavor.
IVORY PRINCESS	Ivory with deep pink-blushed skin and aromatic, intensely sweet, deep cream flesh.
JUNE FLAME	Yellow skin heavily blushed with red. The bright yellow flesh is smooth, juicy, and very sweet. It ripens very well off the tree once it reaches peak color and size and can be eaten firm or juicy.
JUNE LADY	Bright red and gold skin and bright yellow flesh that is exceptionally sweet and juicy when fully tree ripened.
KARLA ROSE	Red-blushed skin with sweet and juicy white flesh.
SPRING LADY	Bright red blush over yellow-orange background, with sweet, juicy yellow flesh.
SPRING SNOW	Pink-blushed cream skin with aromatic, sub-acid white flesh. Very juicy when ripe, but usually picked firm, when crunchy sweet.

BABCOCK	White-fleshed old variety with great-flavored, sweet and juicy, low-acid flesh.
ELEGANT LADY	Yellow-orange mottled with bright red-violet skin, the smooth-textured yellow flesh has the perfect balance of sweet-tart flavor.
SNOW PEACH	A white hybrid with a sweet delicate flavor. Sold by the brand S&W in jars as Snow Peaches.
SUNCREST	This peach was the subject of the novel *Epitaph for a Peach,* written by David Mas Masumoto of Del Rey, California, in 1996, which became a major read for people throughout the world. Masumoto, a writer and farmer, wrote that this delectable, old-fashioned peach was being ripped out in favor of newer breeds. His book triggered a response from growers and this incredibly juicy, highly flavored yellow peach is making a strong comeback.
WHITE LADY	Considered one of the best of the newest hybrid white-fleshed peaches, with a bright red center around the pit. Usually picked firm when crunchy sweet. The mild-flavored, sub-acid flesh will sweeten and become juicy as the fruits ripen off the tree.

AUGUST

CRESTHAVEN	The skin is golden yellow, heavily blushed with bright red. The sweet yellow flesh is bright red around the pit.
DONUT	Two to 3 inches in diameter and only 1½ inches in height, these small, flat peaches have a sunken center. White-fleshed peaches with red-blushed yellow skin, they are intensely sweet and juicy with exceptional flavor. The pit is no larger than a nickel.
O'HENRY	This peach has yellow skin heavily blushed with dark red. The yellow flesh is streaked with red, especially close to the pit. It's great fresh or baked and in canned and frozen forms. However, when picked hard, it does not achieve its potential for flavor and juice. Some of the peaches reach a weight of as much as 1 pound.

SEPTEMBER

CARNIVAL	Yellow with a red blush, this yellow-fleshed peach is one of the latest and is available through early October.
FAIRTIME	The skin is yellow-orange, blushed with bright red. The smooth, firm yellow flesh has a distinctive rich peach flavor. Considered an excellent late-summer variety for pies and home processing.
INDIAN BLOOD CLING PEACH	This blood-red-skinned peach with its flavorful, aromatic orange and sometimes red flesh is sought after for cooking and canning. Its smaller size slides easily into Mason jars, making it desirable for canning whole.
SEPTEMBER SUN, RYAN SUN	Yellow with bright red blush and sweet, juicy yellow flesh, these late-season peaches are picked when tree ripe.

NECTARINES

Variety	Description
MAY	
MAY DIAMOND	Deep red-purple skin with juicy, richly flavored, sweet yellow flesh when fully tree ripened. One of the favorite older varieties at the farmers' markets, along with all the other Diamond varieties, which are known for their deep color and rich flavor.
MAY GRAND	Red and yellow skin with sweet yellow flesh. The flavor is intensely sweet and rich when the fruits are tree ripened and the skin is freckled with sugar dots.
ROSE DIAMOND	Brilliant red skin splashed with gold and richly flavored, candy-sweet yellow flesh make this one of the best of the early-season nectarines.
JUNE	
ARCTIC GLO	New, early-season white nectarine with pink-blushed skin and richly flavored, sweet-tart white flesh providing a perfect balance of sugar and acid.
ARCTIC STAR	Dark red skin and pure white, super-sweet flesh. One of the earliest ripening of the new low-acid, super-sweet white nectarines.
HONEY KIST	One of the new sub-acid yellow nectarines, the shiny skin turns duller when fully ripe. The yellow flesh is intensely sweet even when firm-ripe. Honey Kist has set a record for sweetness at 30 percent sugar when fully tree ripened.
RED DIAMOND	Heavy red blush over yellow skin with deep yellow, richly flavored sweet flesh when tree ripe.
SWEET HOME	A sub-acid, intensely sweet, white-fleshed nectarine named after Paul Buxman's Sweet Home Ranch in California, it has been a top choice for export to Japan and China for more than a decade. The fragrant, cream skin is deeply blushed with red and, like the other intensely sweet peaches, is freckled with sugar dots when ripe. *The Berkeley Wellness Letter* reported that Sweet Home was among the best nectarines tested for nutritional levels.
JULY	
ARCTIC ROSE	Rosy pink blush over white skin with sweet white flesh. Rich flavor and crunchy texture when firm-ripe, it becomes intensely sweet when soft-ripe. Scores high in taste tests.
BRIGHT PEARL	Like many of the other white nectarines, this one gets rave reviews. It has a rosy blush over cream skin with pearl-white flesh that is fragrantly flavorful and dense with sugar. Juicy sweet when fully ripe, these nectarines can be picked firm and will continue to develop sugar off the tree.

DIAMOND RAY	Showing bright red blush over yellow-orange skin and with intensely sweet-tart yellow flesh, the rich flavor of this nectarine is the result of that perfect combination of high sugar and high acid.
FLAVORTOP	Red blush on yellow skin with firm, flavorful sweet flesh. Early harvests produce firm-ripe, tangy-sweet flesh, which turns to a rich sweet flavor in later harvests.
HEAVENLY WHITE	Red blush on cream skin with firm, flavorful, sweet-tart white flesh. The acid–sugar balance gives it a rich and complex flavor that gets high scores in taste tests.
RUBY SWEET	Deep red skin with deep yellow, sub-acid, intensely sweet flesh.
SUMMER GRAND	Bright red blush over golden yellow skin with sweet yellow flesh. Summer Grand has replaced the older Sun Grand variety.

August

ARCTIC BLAZE	Red and cream-white skin with richly flavored, firm, white flesh. Sweet and crisp when harvested early, it becomes intensely sweet when soft-ripe. Scores consistently high in taste tests.
ARCTIC QUEEN	Pink-blushed white skin with richly flavored, super-sweet white flesh. Sweet and crisp when firm-ripe, it becomes intensely sweet when soft-ripe. Scores high in taste tests.
ARCTIC SNOW	One of the season's last whites, it has creamy skin, a floral fragrance, and sweet, crisp flesh.
AUGUST RED	Heavy red blush on yellow skin with intensely flavorful sweet-tart deep yellow flesh.
FLAMEKIST	Red-blushed, bright yellow skin with deep yellow flesh that is sweet and juicy when fully ripe.
ROYAL GIANT	Red blush over yellow skin, which develops to a light russet as the season progresses. The yellow flesh is sweet and juicy when fully ripe.

September

LIZ'S LATE	Red blush on yellow skin with intensely sweet and spicy yellow flesh. Juicy sweet when fully ripe, this is one of the highest-scoring yellow nectarines.
SEPTEMBER RED	Heavy red blush on yellow skin with sweet yellow flesh turning soft and juicy when fully ripe.

PLUMS

Variety	Description
MAY AND JUNE	
RED BEAUT	A sweet and aromatic plum with very juicy, deep yellow flesh and bright to dark red skin that is slightly tart. When fully ripe, Red Beaut is one of the best for eating fresh.
JUNE	
BLACK BEAUT	A large plum with sweet, juicy yellow flesh that turns red as it ripens, while the thick and rather tart skin changes from a deep red to purplish black. Good for cooking and eating fresh.
SANTA ROSA	A juicy plum that sets all standards for the classic sweet-tart flavor. The reddish purple skin encases sweet yellow flesh that turns tangy and red the closer it gets to the stone. Developed by Luther Burbank at his farm in Santa Rosa, California, it ranks high with plum lovers all over the world. Because it goes from hard to overripe in about 24 hours, however, it is no longer grown by large commercial operations. Excellent for eating fresh and a favorite for making jam.
SHIRO	A plum with light yellow skin faintly blushed with red when fully ripe. The sweet, translucent flesh is mild tasting and good for eating fresh. It's also good for cooking if the skin is left on to enhance the flavor.
SHOWTIME	Large with sweet, juicy golden flesh and dark reddish purple skin that is not overly tart. When fully ripe, this is a wonderful plum for eating fresh.
JULY	
BLACK AMBER	As it ripens, the thick skin changes from purple to black while the firm, amber flesh exudes a spicy fragrance. A choice plum for cooking, the dark skin turns the flesh a deep red and adds a pleasingly tart flavor.
EL DORADO	A handsome plum with bright red to reddish black skin tinted with purple and amber flesh that is mildly sweet and juicy-firm. The firm flesh makes this an ideal choice for canning and cooking. Choose fully ripe ones for eating fresh.
METHLEY	A beautiful plum with reddish purple skin and blood-red flesh that is sweet, very juicy, and soft. Good for eating fresh and cooking.
QUEEN ROSA	A large plum with very juicy, mildly sweet, tangy golden flesh. The reddish purple skin is splashed with yellow around the shoulders toward the stem. Enjoyable for eating fresh, it is also a good plum for cooking.
SIMKA	A large plum with tangy-sweet, firm golden flesh and purple skin with red blush. This is an excellent choice for cooking, canning, making into jam, and also eating fresh when fully tree ripened.
WICKSON	Large greenish yellow plum with little tartness in the skin and very sweet, translucent flesh.

BURGUNDY	Spectacular plum with burgundy skin and wine-colored flesh that is very sweet and juicy. With its Bing cherry flavor, it is a favorite for eating fresh and for cooking.
CATALINA	The amber flesh of this large black plum is very sweet, juicy-firm, and intensely flavored when fully ripe. With very little tartness in the skin, it is one of the finest black plums for eating fresh.
ELEPHANT HEART	An extremely large plum with deep red skin and very sweet, juicy crimson flesh. Mildly tart with good flavor, it is one of the best plums for eating fresh. This old plum variety, however, is only available at farmers' markets. It is no longer grown in large commercial orchards.
FORTUNE	As one of the biggest and roundest, it is an impressive looking bright red plum with dense amber flesh that becomes very sweet and juicy when fully tree ripened.
KELSEY	A large, aromatic plum with thin, greenish yellow skin blushed with red when fully ripe. The pale yellow flesh is firm, sweet, and flavorful with no tartness.
LARODA	When fully tree ripened, this is one of the best plums for eating fresh. The sweet amber to red flesh is juicy and bursting with flavor, and the deep reddish purple skin is tender thin and tangy. Also a great plum for cooking and a favorite for making into jam.
NUBIANA	A large plum with a flattened shape and shiny purple-black skin. The firm amber flesh is fragrantly flavorful and sweet with very little tartness. This old-fashioned plum is a top favorite for eating fresh. Its firm flesh also holds up well in cooking.

EMERALD BEAUTY	A greenish yellow skinned plum with sweet yellow-orange flesh that is juicy and crisp.
FRIAR	A large, squat plum with sweet-tart black skin and richly flavored, sweet amber flesh. Friar is harvested firm in July and tree ripe from mid-August to early September. When cooked, the black skin turns the flesh an intense red — hence, this is the plum of Chinese sauce fame.
MARIPOSA	(Improved Satsuma) A flavorful, large plum with mottled deep red and green skin. The red flesh is sweet and juicy-firm. It is delicious for eating fresh and holds up well in cooking.
SATSUMA	Like Mariposa, it has mottled deep red over green skin, and the firm flesh is dark red and very sweet with no tartness. This is an old favorite for eating fresh and making into jam.

ANGELENO	A very large plum with maroon to purple, almost blue, skin. The rich amber flesh is very sweet and dense. When tree ripened, it bursts with flavor. The plum's firm flesh and good keeping qualities enable shipments through Thanksgiving. Wonderful for fresh eating and all cooked dishes.
CASSELMAN	A striking plum with bright red skin and deep amber flesh that is very sweet, deliciously tangy, and dense. Good keeping qualities mean this plum hangs on the trees until November, when it is shipped for Thanksgiving. It is excellent for eating fresh and also holds up well in cooking.

Apricots

Variety	Description
MAY	
AMBERCOT	Medium-sized apricot with yellow-orange skin and firm, sweet flesh.
CASTLEBRITE	Medium-sized apricot with deep yellow skin and firm, full-flavored sweet flesh.
EARLICOT	Large, deep yellow-orange apricot with firm, flavorful flesh.
EARLY GOLDEN	Large, deep yellow apricot with sweet, flavorful flesh.
JORDANNE	Large, deep yellow-orange apricot with intensely flavored flesh.
LORNA	Large, deep orange apricot with sweet, juicy flesh.
POPPY	Medium-large, deep orange apricot with excellent flavor.
ROBADA	Medium-sized apricot with red-blushed, yellow-orange skin and exceptionally sweet, juicy flesh.
JUNE	
BLENHEIM	Small to medium apricot with pale orange skin and lusciously sweet, juicy, intensely flavored flesh.
CHINESE SWEET	Medium-sized, heart-shaped orange apricot with intensely sweet flesh.
GOLDBAR	Medium, yellow-orange skin with deep red blush and firm, flavorful, sweet flesh.
HELENA	Large, golden-yellow apricot with firm, flavorful, juicy flesh.
MOORPARK	Large, orange apricot with slightly juicy, firm flesh that is exceptionally flavorful, sweet, and aromatic. A favorite apricot for the fresh market, it is also grown for commercial canning and drying.
PATTERSON	Medium-sized, golden-yellow apricot with firm, flavorful sweet flesh.
TOMCOT	Large, orange apricot with sweet firm flesh.
TRIGEM	Large, deep-yellow apricot with firm, flavorful flesh.
JULY	
AUTUMN GLO	Large, deep-yellow apricot with soft sweet flesh.
HARGLOW	Medium-sized apricot with red-blushed orange skin and firm, flavorful, sweet orange flesh. A favorite apricot of growers in coastal northwestern climates.
TILTON	Large, golden-orange apricot with firm, flavorful, sweet-tart flesh. A favorite of the fresh market, its firm flesh also makes it a top commercial choice for canning and drying.
VEECOT	Medium-large, round apricot with deep-orange color and firm, slightly juicy flesh.

Aprium

Variety	Description
June	
FLAVOR DELIGHT	This aprium has yellow skin and flesh as well as a sweet, distinctive flavor.
HONEY RICH	Marked by bright yellow shiny skin and juicy sweet, semitransparent flesh.

Plumcot

Variety	Description
May/June	
FLAVORELLA	Orange-yellow, velvety skin and bright yellow flesh with intense sweet-tart flavor. To date, this is the main plumcot variety in widespread commercial production.
FLAVORGLO	Orange-yellow skin and yellow tart-sweet flesh.
EDEN PRIDE	More heart shaped than round, it has orange skin blushed with red and yellow-orange flesh that is intensely sweet and tart.

Pluot

Variety	Description
June	
FLAVOROSA	Flattened shape with dark purple skin and sweet red flesh.
FLAVOR SUPREME	Mottled red over green skin with sweet, firm red flesh. It was the first commercial pluot, introduced 1989 by breeder Floyd Zaiger, who nicknamed it Ugly Duckling.
FRUIT PUNCH	Heart shaped with clear pink skin and juicy flesh with sweet, grapelike flavor.
Mid-July through August	
DAPPLE DANDY	Pinkish skin with maroon and yellow dapple; resembles a large speckled egg. The plum-and-apricot-flavored red-flecked flesh is very sweet and juicy. Also marketed as Dinosaur Egg.
FLAVOR QUEEN	Pale yellow skin with juicy. candy-sweet yellow-orange flesh.
August	
FLAVOR HEART	Heart shaped with purple-black skin and sweet yellow flesh.
FLAVOR KING	Purple-red skin with sweet, spicy flesh that moves from bright red under the skin to yellow orange as it nears the pit. Considered one of the most sensationally flavored pluots developed to date.
FLAVOR RICH	Purple-black skin and firm yellow-orange flesh; sweet plum favor with a zingy apricot finish.

RESOURCES

Restaurants

Bishop's Restaurant
2183 West 4th Avenue
Vancouver, British Columbia V6K 1N7
(604) 738-2025
www.bishopsonline.com
(*Simply Bishop's: Easy Seasonal Recipes*,
Douglas & McIntyre, Vancouver, 2003)

McCrady's Restaurant
2 Unity Alley
Charleston, SC 29401
(843) 577-0025; fax: (843) 577-3681
www.mccradysrestaurant.com

Mail Order

Dickey Farms
P.O. Box 10
Musella, GA 31066
(478) 8366-4362, (800) 732-2442;
fax: (478) 836 2966
E-mail: info@gapeaches.com
www.gapeaches.com
Fresh peaches.

Douglas Fruit
110 Taylor Flats Road
Pasco, WA 99301
(509) 543-9356; fax: (509) 543-9357
E-mail: cindy@douglasfruit.com
www.douglasfruit.com
Fresh apricots, peaches, and nectarines.

Durbin Farms
130 7th Street South
Clanton, AL 35045
(877) 818-0202; fax: (205) 755-9589
E-mail: office@durbinfarms.com
www.durbinfarms.com
Fresh peaches, nectarines, and plums.

Eden Garden
Tracy, CA 95304
(888) 882-7742
E-mail: edngrdn@pacbell.net
www.edengarden.com
*Fruit of the month: apricots, apriums,
pluots and plumcots; also chocolate-
dipped fruits, pluots.*

Fresh Fruit Delivered
P.O. BOX 927
Quincy, WA 98848
(888) 535-1561; fax: 509-787-6163
E-mail: shad@freshfruitdelivered.com
www.freshfruitdelivered.com
*Peaches, nectarines, plums (Japanese,
Italian, and damsons).*

Goldbud Farms
Placerville, CA
(530) 626-6521
*Fresh Indian blood peaches, white
nectarines, and peaches.*

Gonzales Orchards
Hollister, CA 95023
(831) 637-1938; fax: (831) 637-4636
E-mail: info@apricotking.com
Dried and fresh apricots, jams, and syrups.

Great Country Farms
18780 Foggy Bottom Road
Bluemont, VA 20134
(540) 554-2073; fax: (540) 554-2073
E-mail: farmers@dsdial.net
www.greatcountryfarms.com
Fresh peaches, plums, and apricots.

Harry and David
P.O. Box 712
Medford, OR 97501
(800) 345-5655; fax: (800) 648-6640
www.harryanddavid.com
*Dried fruits, chocolate-dipped fruits,
and fresh yellow peaches.*

Honeycrisp Farm
9400 South Lac Jac Road
Reedley, CA 93650
(559) 638-3084
www.honeycrispfarm.com
*Dried and fresh white nectarines
and peaches.*

J. E. Cooley Farms
3097 State 11 West
Chesnee, SC 29323
(864) 461-7225
*Peach farm, restaurant and ice-cream
parlor (homemade peach ice cream).*

Mariani Farm & Packing
Company
500 Crocker Drive
Vacaville, CA 95688-8706
(800) 672-8655
E-mail:
productinfo@marianipacking.com
www.marianipacking.com
*Dried and fresh plums, pluots, peaches,
and apricots.*

McCleod Farms
State 151 South & US 1 North
McBee, SC 29101
(843) 335-8611
www.macspride.com
Fresh peaches.

Stewart and Jasper Orchards
3500 Shiells Road
Neuman, CA 95360
(209) 862-9600; fax: (209) 862-9611
E-mail: sales@stewartandjasper.com
www.stewardandjasper.com
Fresh white peaches and nectarines;
pluots, plumcots, and apricots.

Fruit and Food Associations

Agricultural Research Magazine
5601 Sunnyside Avenue
Beltsville, MD 20705-5130
(301) 504-1651

Apricot Producers of California
2111 Geer Road, Suite 611
Turlock, CA 95382
(209) 632-9777; fax: (209) 632-9779
www.apricotproducers.com

California Canning Peach
Association
2300 River Plaza Drive, Suite 110
Sacramento, CA 95833
(916) 925-9131; fax: (916) 925-9030

California Clean
The Agrarian Advocate
P.O. Box 363
Davis, CA 95617
www.californiaclean.com

California Department of Food &
Agriculture
1220 North Street, Suite 409
P.O. Box 942871
Sacramento, CA 94271-0001
(916) 654-0433; fax: (916) 654-0403
www.cdfa.ca.gov

California Dried Plum Board
P.O. Box 348180
Sacramento, CA 95834
(916) 565-6232; fax: (916) 565-6237
www.californiadriedplums.org

California Fresh Apricot Council
19 Sherwood Court
San Francisco, CA 94127
(415) 584-4063; fax (415) 584-3834
www.califapricot.com

California Tree Fruit Agreement
975 I Street
P.O. Box 968
Reedley, CA 93654-0968
(559) 638-8260; fax: (559) 638-8842
www.caltreefruit.com

Georgia Department of
Agriculture
Agriculture Building, Room 204
Capitol Square
Atlanta, GA 30334-2001
(404) 656-3600; fax: (404) 651-7957
www.agr.state.ga.us

Luther Burbank Home & Gardens
(docent- and self-guided tours)
P.O. Box 1678
Santa Rosa, CA 95402
(707) 524-5445; fax: (707) 524-5827
www.lutherburbank.org

National Association of State
Department of Agriculture
1156 15th Street NW, Suite 1020
Washington, DC 20005
(202) 296-9680; fax: (202) 296-9686

Produce for Better Health
Foundation
5301 Limestone Road, Suite 101
Wilmington, DE 19808-1249
www.5aday.com

South Carolina Department
of Agriculture
Wade Hampton Office Building
P.O. Box 11280
Columbia, SC 29211-1280
(803) 734-2190; fax: (803) 734-2192

United Fresh Fruit & Vegetable
Association
1901 Pennsylvania Avenue NW
Suite 1100
Washington, DC 20006
(202) 303-3400; fax: (202) 303-3433
www.uffva.org

University of Georgia
Mark Rieger
Professor of Horticulture
1111 Plant Sciences
Athens, GA 30602
(706) 542-0783; fax: (706) 542-0624
www.uga.edu/fruit

Zaiger's Genetics
1219 Grimes Avenue
Modesto, CA 95358
(209) 522-1075
www.davewilson.com

INDEX